FAILURE FACTORY

How Baltimore City Public Schools Deprive
Taxpayers and Students of a Future

CHRIS PAPST

**RADIO
FREE
PRESS**

an imprint of Sunbury Press, Inc.
Mechanicsburg, PA USA

RADIO FREE PRESS

an imprint of Sunbury Press, Inc.
Mechanicsburg, PA USA

For information about special discounts for bulk purchases, please contact Sunbury Press Orders Dept. at (855) 338-8359 or orders@sunburypress.com.

To request one of our authors for speaking engagements or book signings, please contact Sunbury Press Publicity Dept. at publicity@sunburypress.com.

FIRST RADIO FREE PRESS EDITION: August 2025

Set in Adobe Garamond | Interior design by Crystal Devine | Cover by Lawrence Knorr | Edited by Leah Brennsteiner.

Publisher's Cataloging-in-Publication Data
Names: Papst, Chris, author.
Title: Failure factory : how Baltimore City public schools deprive taxpayers and students of a future / Chris Papst.
Description: First trade paperback edition. | Mechanicsburg, PA : Radio Free Press, 2025.
Summary: Baltimore City Public Schools is one of America's largest and most funded school systems. Yet, historically, it's among the lowest performing. In 2024, despite a $1.7 billion budget, just 10% of students tested proficient in math. Investigative journalist Chris Papst follows the money to uncover why students keep failing within a school system that's failing Baltimore.
Identifiers: ISBN 979-8-88819-350-1 (hardcover) | ISBN 979-8-88819-349-5 (softcover).
Subjects: EDUCATION / Administration / Elementary & Secondary | POLITICAL SCIENCE / American Government / Local | BUSINESS & ECONOMICS / Accounting / Governmental.

Designed in the USA
0 1 1 2 3 5 8 13 21 34 55

For the Love of Books!

Voicemails, emails, and quotes are presented verbatim, without edits.

Chris Papst is a National Emmy award-winning investigative reporter and the 2023 Maryland State Conference NAACP Vanguard Award recipient.

"If you want to see the poor remain poor, generation after generation, just keep the standards low in their schools and make excuses for their academic shortcomings and personal misbehavior."

—THOMAS SOWELL
2002 National Humanities Medal Recipient

CONTENTS

ACKNOWLEDGMENTS

This project would not have been possible without the encouragement and loving support of my wife, family and close friends. To my news managers whose vision and advocacy shaped this unique brand of relentless investigative reporting, know you are appreciated. And to all the members of Project Baltimore, thank you.

Go Team!

FOREWORD

In his book, *Failure Factory*, Chris Papst explores a topic vital to the survival of a city and state, both socially and economically—education. Specifically, that of Baltimore City Public Schools. In his writing, Papst provides the public with a lens by which to capture the internal functions of the district, portraying both failures and successes. There are those who argue and try to dismiss the reporting on realities in educational systems, such as that featured in this book, as incendiary and exacerbating to the current issues without resolving them. Mr. Papst views the positive and negative aspects of the situation. Using personal anecdotes, he provides insight that extends far beyond what is often afforded to the public, into the mechanisms of education. Accordingly, the facts put forth in this book consistently underlie the case for necessary reforms in education, for the welfare of all students.

Papst provides a factual basis for the assertions expressed in the book. His documentation is based on intense investigations over eight years. And, whether some critics would acknowledge it or not, his descriptions reflect not just the current educational occurrences in one major city, but what is happening across the nation. When considered proactively, rather than reactively, he provides readers the opportunity to analyze negative circumstances impacting students in order to collaborate and develop solutions, as an informed public. To that end, Papst's text furnishes what is often missing in communication between school districts and their vulnerable clients: transparency.

All parents, whether classified as majority or minority, bring their children to the schoolhouse door and trust those in charge to educate them to help fulfill their futures, even in ways that parents themselves cannot. Yet too often that promise is not kept, and the trust in the system breaks down. In his analysis, Papst makes clear that determining solutions can only be accomplished as a joint effort, across constituencies and involving multiple segments of the community. Simply, he poses that this is no time for those in authority to become defensive; rather, it is past time to come to the defense of those who are most vulnerable and voiceless—the children. Along that vein, Mr. Papst provides a voice to parents who have too frequently been sidelined or totally marginalized.

Failure Factory does not call for the annihilation of education systems. It does demand recognizing what is not working or simply wrong and then pursuing corrections. Educational institutions have evolved into a new bureaucracy. We must sometimes wonder what happened with the sacred mission—when was it sacrificed and to what purpose? The issues surrounding minorities and the impoverished not being adequately educated have gone on for over a century. The matters get more focus today, basically due to mass media and the Web. And frankly, some don't like what they see. Now, via this book, the public can observe closely the faulty practices, ineffective workarounds, and the solutions that don't work, but continuously get repackaged for public consumption.

Throughout his writing, Chris Papst goes beyond simply providing a single-blame narration for decades of underachievement. He challenges parents and the public in general to act against the laissez-faire attitude toward the education of children, which has increased particularly in recent years. Although he speaks to parental responsibility and engagement, Mr. Papst steadily rebuts the allegation that parents should bear inordinate blame for academic failure. Is it fair to blame parents for their children's lack of educational success, when many parents themselves were undereducated by the same school system their children now attend?

As a journalist, Papst demonstrates the courage to challenge powerful bureaucracies by holding those at the top accountable. He also rejects the premise that the reason for a lack of appropriate education is due to parents and students themselves, based on their living conditions. Although those factors play a role, they are not insurmountable. After all, school systems receive billions of tax dollars intended for the sole purpose of educating students, not some students, but all students. And that mission should not be predicated on the environment from which the students leave when they enter the schoolhouse.

In addition to the intense scrutiny of achievement among students and academic challenges among minorities and the poor, Papst also deeply explores topics such as grading, promotions, discipline, school safety, and violence while providing cogent examples. Through the book and its stories, Papst raises questions about whether or not the situation is truly the failure of children or the failure of systems to address their needs. Is this phenomenon due to the students failing academically or the way in which they are being educated? In other words, are children failing school, or are schools failing children?

Barbara Dezmon, Ph.D.
Education Committee Chair: Maryland State Conference NAACP
(2010–2023)

PROLOGUE

The Circuit Court for Baltimore City, Maryland

Date:
Monday, February 11, 2019

Case Number:
24-C-17-006516
Fox45 News/Project Baltimore vs. Baltimore City Board of
School Commissioners

BEFORE:
HONORABLE JEANNIE J. HONG, ASSOCIATE JUDGE

APPEARANCES:
For the Plaintiff:
SCOTT H. MARDER, ESQUIRE

For the Defendant:
TAMAL A. BANTON, ESQUIRE

Electronic Proceedings Transcribed by: Nicole M. Kittleson

Video of Proceedings Prohibited

PLAINTIFF'S WITNESSES:
Chris Papst

PROCEEDINGS
(9:33 a.m.)

MR. MARDER: Your Honor, I'll put Mr. Papst on the stand.

THE COURT: Okay. Mr. Papst, please come to the witness stand.

THE CLERK: Please remain standing and raise your right hand. Do you solemnly affirm that the evidence you shall give shall be the truth, the whole truth, and nothing but the truth?

MR. PAPST: I DO.

THE CLERK: Thank you. You may lower your hand. You may be seated. Sir, please speak directly into the microphone. State your full name for the record.

THE WITNESS: Chris Papst.

DIRECT EXAMINATION
BY MR. MARDER:

Q Good morning, Mr. Papst.
A Morning.
Q Where do you work?
A I work for Fox45 News.
Q And what is your job with Fox45?
A We have an investigative unit called Project Baltimore and I'm the reporter for that unit.
Q How long have you been an investigative reporter?
A Probably about six years or so.
Q And how long have you been with Fox45?
A I've been working at Fox45 for more than two years.
Q And can you tell the Court just a little bit about your educational background?

A   I received a Bachelors of Arts from University of Pittsburgh and a Masters of Arts from Temple University in Philadelphia.

Q   Now, Mr. Papst, what is Project Baltimore?

A   Project Baltimore was designed as a long-term investigative unit that would focus on one topic over a series of years. The first topic we picked was education in the Baltimore area which has also kind of morphed into education in Maryland as a whole. How money is spent, test scores, violence in schools, bullying, teacher credentials. We look at the gamut of anything that would be involved in education.

Q   During the course of working on Project Baltimore, approximately how much time have you spent reviewing data about performance of the Baltimore City Public Schools?

A   A lot.

Q   Hundreds of hours?

A   I mean, I would say --

MR. BANTON: Objection. Objection. Leading.
THE COURT: I'm sorry?
MR. BANTON: Leading.
THE COURT: Denied.

Q   My question is, Mr. Papst, how much time have you spent researching and investigating statistics about the performance of Baltimore City Public Schools?

A   I would say when we started more than two years ago, that was probably the first thing that we looked into, so it's been more than two years on a steady basis. Probably every week, at some point, I'm looking at data concerning the school systems. Whether it's graduation rates, test scores, other performance measures.

Q   Has the Baltimore City Schools put out statistics on performance of its students?

A   Yes.

Q And, for instance, in the last year in which you had statistics available from the city schools, what were the PARCC (state testing/proficiency) rates, PARCC literacy rates, indicated by the Baltimore City Public Schools?

MR. BANTON: Objection.
THE COURT: Basis?
MR. BANTON: Relevance.
THE COURT: Overruled.

A There's many test scores that you can look at. There's not one individual test score and you can't give one number for an entire school system. But if you look at 3rd to 8th grade, for example, Baltimore City's proficiency rates are somewhere around 15 to 16 percent in math and English, and the State averages are around the mid 40s.

Q Now, how about at the Baltimore City school called NACA II?

A They had zero proficiency in math when we were conducting the initial investigation in 2017 into that school. So when we looked them up, their math proficiency rates were zero. There was not one high school student in that school that was proficient in math.

Q During the course of your investigation, did you ever receive any information about grade-changing allegations in the Baltimore City schools?

MR. BANTON: Objection. Leading.
THE COURT: Overruled.

Q Tell us about what you learned.

A We had numerous teachers come to us saying that the grades they had submitted for their students were not the final grades that the students received. The teachers had said to us they're not sure how these students graduated. The teachers that we had spoken to were involved in classes that these students needed to graduate. They came to us with the report cards and with the grades for those students and said, "I don't know how this child could have graduated. I was his teacher in this class. He needs this class to graduate. He did not pass the class, but yet the student graduated."

Q Now, after receiving that information, what did you do?
A We interviewed the teachers.
Q Understood, and did you ever send anything to the Baltimore City Public Schools?
A We had requested interviews from them to talk about the allegations these teachers had made. We had reached out to the school itself, NACA II.

Q I am going to show you what has been marked as Plaintiff's Exhibit No. 1 for identification. Is that the first public records request that you submitted to the school, to the school board, about this subject?
A Yes. This is the request I had sent specific to NACA II for the results of their internal grade-changing investigation, which was launched following our reporting into the school.

Q Please take a look at the next Plaintiff's Exhibit for identification. Do you recognize this?
A This is City School's response to the second public records request we sent asking for the results and any and all documentation collected for all internal grade-changing investigations conducted by City Schools since 2010.
Q Mr. Papst, what did the school board offer to give you following your public records requests.
A Nothing.

MR. BANTON: Objection. Leading.
THE COURT: Overruled.

Q Prior to Fox45 filing suit in this case, did City Schools provide you with any documents in response to your two MPIA requests?
A Nothing.

CHAPTER 1

"WINNERS AND LOSERS"

If you have visited West Baltimore lately, you understand. If you haven't, you can't understand. But I'll try to explain what it's like and then offer an argument for how it got that way.

The drive through this section of the city is memorable, perhaps unforgettable. These streets are literally littered with fantastic images of charm and prestige. It's block after block of three-story, brick and stone row homes. Each one, gabled with wood moldings and carved granite. White marble steps and oak doors add a nice local touch to the Federal-style construction. Every few blocks, the homes expand into sprawling parks or colonial mansions set on manicured lots. It's gorgeous. Or at least it was in 1925.

The 2025 version of West Baltimore looks a bit different. Plywood has replaced glass as the preferred window dressing. Most of the crown molding has rotted. What's left of the marble steps has sunk into the ground. The shade trees that once lined the sidewalks have been cut down, I was told to allow police helicopters to better track fleeing suspects. The pavement that those trees once covered with leaves is now covered with trash. If you do see a tree, it's likely growing out of an abandoned home. In this area, there are very few grocery stores. Or any type of store, for that matter. But what is common are balloons. Every couple of blocks, you'll notice some tied to a stop sign or fire hydrant. But these are not balloons of celebration. They are temporary shrines of commemoration—often surrounded by burnt-out candles, family pictures, and the occasional teddy bear.

Baltimore's population, according to the U.S. Census, was higher in 1920 than it was in 2020. Many good people are fighting to improve the city's quality of life and convince residents to stay. But it's a struggle. In 2024, Baltimore was named the deadliest city in America by SafeHome. And West Baltimore is perhaps the deadliest section.

But it's not just West Baltimore that's beset by blight. Much of the city has fallen into a state of decay. And that was certainly my view one September afternoon in 2017, as my photographer and I were heading to Calverton Elementary/Middle School to try to speak with the principal.

"I know I say this every time we come into the city . . ." My photographer's eyes glanced over at me. But he didn't bother to turn his head.

"Baltimore has so much potential," I said, staring out the window.

Early October in Maryland can go either way. It can be hot and sunny or cold and dreary. This day was somewhere in the middle.

"How do you want to handle this?" He asked, handing me a microphone.

I glanced down at my phone, double-checking the bell schedule.

"Once all the students are gone, we'll walk up to the school and ring the doorbell. I'm assuming it has a doorbell." I had no idea. "Then, we wait."

He lowered his visor to block the dropping sun. "Do they know we're coming?"

I clipped the mic onto my tie and stuffed the wire into my shirt. "They should."

"How long before we get kicked off?" His question was more of a statement.

I peered over at the large-bodied, lightly groomed, West Virginian— the eastern panhandle type, not the deep woods type. "We might have a few minutes."

Calverton's principal was proving elusive. For weeks, we had been trying to get a hold of her. We had lots of questions. But she gave us nothing. And getting "nothing" for a journalist is very motivating.

Calverton Elementary/Middle resembled any other 1960s-era American school. Red brick, metal doors, and plenty of concrete. Classrooms to the left. A large, square gymnasium to the right. And crammed in the middle was a lobby and a small office. It had no air conditioning and a history of being poorly maintained. A few months after our visit, in January of 2018, a severe cold snap broke the school's heating and plumbing systems. All 650 students were forced into other District buildings for two weeks.

On this day, however, Calverton was open and had just dismissed when we arrived. As my photographer and I approached the school and parked, we could see it had largely emptied. Just a few students remained.

"You ready?" he asked, cleaning his lens. Before we left the office, we situated our gear in the front seat. Cameras, lights, microphones, batteries. Once that car was parked, we needed to move. News spreads quickly when a TV reporter is spotted holding a microphone—especially at a school. Once the photographer throws that huge camera on his shoulder, there's no turning back. And if we get discovered too early, we can lose our story.

I quickly reviewed my questions written on a paper tablet. "Alright," I sighed with a nod. Reaching down, I pulled the door handle. "Here we go."

* * *

The front doors of Calverton were about 40 yards from the sidewalk, which is a problem when a TV reporter is attempting an "unscheduled interview." My photographer leaned out of the car and hoisted the camera. We shut the car doors and started walking.

Trespassing laws in Maryland (and many other states) are a little tricky concerning public schools. They are considered "public buildings." They are bought and maintained by tax dollars. But government officials have the authority to remove members of the public. And the media have no special status. We're allowed on the property until we're told to leave. There is some nuance to the law. It's not quite that rigid. But when students could possibly be around, the nuance narrows.

"You ready?" I asked my photographer as we approached the school. He nodded.

At this point, we had already been spotted by many students, parents, and employees. The walk up to the school was simply too long.

The front doors of Calverton were gray steel, with thin rectangular windows. I peered inside. The hallways were empty.

"I'm going to ring the doorbell."

The reply came from behind the camera, "Rolling."

When I pressed the button, I didn't hear anything. No chimes. No beep. After about a minute, I pressed it again. Nothing. I wasn't sure if I was being ignored or if the doorbell was broken. In Baltimore, you never know.

Based on experience, I assumed that by now, the principal was already calling the central office asking for help. So, I rang the doorbell again. Still nothing. We waited three or four minutes. A small and curious crowd began to form on the street. But there was no movement inside the school.

This was not what I expected. I assumed, after a few minutes or so, someone would tell me to leave through the intercom. Or perhaps we'd get the obligatory, "no comment." Perhaps the doorbell was actually broken.

"What now?" my photographer asked. The camera remained on his shoulder, recording.

I shrugged. "Is it worth standing here longer?"

"If they were going to do something," he replied, "they would have done it by now."

I nodded. "Let's wait on the sidewalk. One of those cars may be the principal's," I specifically gestured towards the new Acura. In Baltimore City, the median income in 2017 was about $29,000, among the lowest in Maryland. But principals could make north of $160,000, among the highest in Maryland. It's a disparity that certainly breeds resentment, especially if your child can't read by high school.

Walking towards the street, the small crowd dispersed. It appeared nothing interesting was going to happen. Then, with a loud thud that echoed through the surrounding blight, the deadbolt of the metal door released.

"Hey!" A uniformed Baltimore City Schools Police Officer emerged from the door. "You need to leave," he loudly commanded.

Baltimore City Schools Police are sworn officers; they attend the same academy as the Baltimore City Police. The difference is that they aren't allowed to carry their guns inside a school. They are the only officers in Maryland who must disarm themselves while inside a city school. They can be armed while off duty or outside the building on district property. But as soon as they walk into a school, their gun goes into a locker.

This particular officer had a gun on his hip. We must have been a threat.

"We can't be on school grounds?" I asked, walking towards him.

"No, you cannot." He slowed his approach and angled himself away from the camera.

I proceeded politely, "Ok, we're just going to stand here on the sidewalk."

That must have been the wrong answer.

"You cannot stand on the sidewalk, either." He hastened his approach. "It's Baltimore City policy, you cannot be on school grounds. You can stand on the other side of the street."

"Sir," I replied calmly, "the sidewalk is public property. It's not school property. You can ask me to leave school grounds, but you cannot ask me to leave the sidewalk."

The uniformed officer was now standing right in front of me. "I'm not going to debate with you. I'm not. I don't make the rules, I just enforce them."

He backed me into a decision. "So, we have to go to the other side of the street?"

"Yes," he responded with a hand gesture. "The other side of the street."

I turned that way. "Ok."

I saw no need to escalate the situation. His mere presence kept the story alive. Plus, our questions were for the principal. Not him. I also knew what was coming next. And a few minutes later, my phone rang.

"Christopher. What are you doing now?"

Edie House was Baltimore City Schools' long-time public information officer, or PIO. In my line of work, relationships with PIOs can get a bit contentious. Edie was different. She was a former TV reporter. She understood I was doing my job. And I understood she was doing hers.

"I was just kicked off a sidewalk. That's a first," I replied. "I'm standing outside Calverton."

She was quick. "I know! I've gotten 10 calls in the last five minutes. Quit causing me trouble. It's the end of the day."

I chuckled. "The police officer told us the sidewalk is not public."

She sighed. "Ok. I'll call the school."

"You know, Edie," I heard her sigh again, "I wouldn't have to do this if the school system would speak with me."

"Christopher." She said my name like a grandmother. "I should be on my way home. I have a nice bottle of red wine waiting for me." She took a slow breath. "Just stay on the sidewalk."

The line went dead.

* * *

We went to Calverton that day because we had received complaints that the school was changing failing grades to passing to promote students to the next grade. This was something we had heard from parents at several city schools. One of those parents was Gregory Gray.

Gray was a 44-year-old Baltimore native. Short and thin with a shaved head, he struck me as a man who had a challenging life. But now, he was focused on his son. Gray didn't feel the school system was preparing his son for a life better than his own. When we interviewed Gray, his son was a fifth grader at Mount Royal Elementary in Midtown.

"He's a short little guy for his age, you wouldn't think he's 12. He's small," explained Gray with a loving smile. We interviewed him and his son at a playground. "He's just like any other kid, just wants to have fun. Sometimes he's misunderstood. Sometimes he can be mischievous." He laughed as his son swung awkwardly on the bars. "He's just a very energetic kid, and he's very smart. Very, very smart."

Gray told us the school system was passing his son through the grades regardless of his test scores or work ethic. And this father knew his son was smart enough to figure that out.

"It's like Martin Luther King said," explained Gray, "if you see wrongdoing, if you see injustice, and you don't say nothing about it, you more guilty than the person that's doing the injustice."

Parents like Gray are common in Baltimore. This is a school system where as few as seven percent of all students, in third through eighth grade, test proficient in math (Yes, SEVEN percent). Yet, the graduation rate hovers around 70 percent.

Parents like Gray try to challenge the school system. But they feel powerless. This is a district with a $1.7 billion budget. Meanwhile, many Baltimore parents depend on government assistance to survive. Plus, this city has taken a lot from its people.

When I first got to Baltimore in early 2017, I didn't understand the extent to which this community had suffered. I'm not sure anyone can understand who hasn't directly experienced it.

I would say I've lived a normal American life. I grew up about 45 minutes west of Philadelphia in a quiet farm town—fishing, football, and four-wheel drives. I was educated in the public school system and raised by two devoted and loving parents.

I earned a scholarship to play baseball for four years at the University of Pittsburgh. Then, I earned my master's degree at Temple University. Shortly after that, I got married and began building a career in journalism. Then came a yellow lab, kids and a mortgage. Those are the basic experiences that shaped my life and personality.

Extreme violence is something I never experienced until I began this career. Covering murders, non-fatal shootings, and carjackings is newsworthy because it's relatively rare throughout America. But in Baltimore, violence is far more common. Up until I entered this career, I didn't know one person who had been murdered. I've never dealt with that level of trauma or sudden, unnecessary loss. But in Baltimore, it's hard to find someone who hasn't experienced losing a loved one in such a way.

A few months before we interviewed Gray, his close family friend was shot and killed. He was one of the 1,672 people murdered in Baltimore from 2017 to 2021. Those five years constitute the deadliest five years in the city's nearly 300-year history. With a murder rate of 59 per 100,000 residents, this city recorded a homicide rate as high as 12 times the U.S. national average.

During our interview, when Gray spoke about his friend, it clearly affected him. Yet, he remained composed. But when he expressed the impact the murder had on his son, Gray broke down. "He took it real hard." The man's dark brown eyes were fixed on the ground. "He had this mentality like, 'Dad, I'm not going to let nobody get me first.' And I used to have to tell my son, 'that's not cool.'"

The mental anguish his son endured following the murder led to his acting out in school. He was given an individualized education program, or IEP, to provide him with extra support. But Gray says his son never got the tutoring he needed. What his son needed was help. Instead, the boy was just passed to the next grade.

"My son is really in desperate need of tutoring in math." Gray's mourning turned to anger and frustration. "How did my son pass if he didn't know none of this math? They passed them, they just passed them along. He didn't know the material."

He paused to find the words.

"They had to change his grade." He shook his head. "I just wanted my son to learn his math because you need math, you need an education. It's very important. It's very important. I'm disgusted with Baltimore City Schools."

* * *

As Project Baltimore's investigation into grade-fixing allegations at Calverton and other schools intensified, word began to spread through the community. This was a topic people had often discussed in this city. But the local media never really dug into it. We started to hear from many people who claimed students' grades were being improperly changed to pass them to the next grade. One of those people was a teacher at Calverton.

It's rare that we hear from teachers who've been in the system for many years. However, when we began airing our investigation into grade changing, we did interview one long-time teacher who said, "That is not news. When I heard your stories, I wondered why anybody is shocked. We have graduated kids who can't read."

Most of the teacher interviews we get are with young or new teachers, who have not yet become normalized to the standards of the system. And that was the case with the educator from Calverton.

This Calverton teacher had recently graduated from college and, like most, had noble aspirations to improve the lives of inner-city youth. This mindset describes many young teachers I meet who are new to Baltimore. But when they get to the city, the bureaucracy begins to wear many of them down. The established system operates in a way where many new teachers often can't make the positive impact that they dreamt of. After a year or two, frustration sets in. Most new teachers recognize the system is omnipotent, and they either quit, conform, or just stay quiet. Others refuse to acquiesce. Those are usually the educators who contact me.

We met the Calverton teacher after school at Fox45 News studios. We snuck them in through a side door to ensure anonymity. In the teacher's mind, they were trying to do the right thing by blowing the whistle on a perceived injustice. But this educator also knew they'd lose their job if outed.

We set up in an old studio. Our cameras were focused on the brightly lit studio equipment in the background. The teacher sat in a foreground chair, unfocused, in black silhouette. A hooded sweatshirt masked the true outline of their head and shoulders.

Investigative TV journalists don't like doing silhouetted interviews. We are a visual medium that relies on establishing an emotional connection with the viewers. If the audience cannot see the interviewee's eyes or hear their natural voice, that connection cannot easily be made. But in this case, there was no other way to get this teacher on camera. We agreed to conceal their identity because we didn't want to jeopardize their job. Plus, we didn't necessarily need this person's emotion to tell the story. This educator had something else we were after.

This is the actual transcript from the interview.

Reporter Transcript: October 18, 2017

Papst: As a teacher at Calverton, you received that text?

Calverton Teacher: Yes.

Papst: What was that text telling you to do?

Calverton Teacher: Go into my grade book, make sure no students are failing, and essentially change the grade if they are failing so they will pass with a 60 percent.

Papst: When you got that text, what did you think?

Calverton Teacher: I was frustrated as a teacher because it's my job to make sure my students are learning, and it's also my job to make sure they are held accountable if they are not doing what they need to do in the classroom. For many students, grades are important to them. When they see they are able to pass without doing anything in the classroom, or without being in the classroom, that sends a message that is completely opposite as what I want to send as a teacher.

Calverton Teacher: There was definitely teacher pushback. But there's also limits to what teachers can do. If you speak up, you become a target. So a lot of people don't speak up.

Papst: Did anybody go to North Avenue to say, hey, grades are being changed at Calverton, here's a text from our principal telling us to change grades?

Calverton Teacher: Not to my knowledge. I think a lot of people are afraid of losing their jobs. People are scared at Calverton. Teachers are scared. People are afraid to do what is best for the kids because they're afraid of losing their jobs. I can only assume this is something that happens across the District.

Papst: How common in your experience is grade changing at Calverton?

Calverton Teacher: Very common. Just about every nine weeks, it would become an issue because report cards come out, because we needed to show students passing according to administration. Students could skip class every day. Run in the hall every day. Not do work every day. Not be suspended. And still pass with 60s on their report cards. Everyday life. It's a struggle because you want to do so much for the kids. You feel powerless at the end of the day when factors like grades are out of your control, regardless of what you do. It also damages the children who work really hard. They are seeing their peers getting by doing little to nothing. That's discouraging.

Calverton Teacher: I feel very passionate about the students who attend the school and they are not having an experience that's typical for elementary and middle school students who are learning life skills, such as accountability, and with grade changing, students are not being held accountable to their actions in school and they are not learning life skills. This is something that a lot of teachers know about at Calverton, and that has been ongoing at the school.

End Reporter Transcript: October 18, 2017

The text message I asked the teacher about was sent by Calverton's principal, Martia Cooper. All of the teachers at the school received it, minus the secretary's name, which is redacted. Here's the exact text as it was sent on June 13, 2017:

> Good Morning people! (Redacted) is printing report cards so finally you can get cumes finished. Please double check end of year averages and make sure they are 60 and above, except our four retention candidates (2 elem and 2 grade 7). If you find any grade averages below 60, pkesss [*sic*] have (Redacted) correct and give me a copy of those student names. Thanks!

"We're public servants," the teacher told us during the interview. "And when we see things like grade changing, that's self-serving. That's not helping the kids. Teaching a whole generation of kids that they don't have to be accountable for their actions, or that hard work isn't valued or valuable when they are in school, is so discouraging and damaging."

That text was just one piece of our investigation into Calverton. We also had something perhaps even more damning—documents which seemed to prove grade changing was happening. The documents were given to us by a high-level source within Baltimore City Schools' administrative headquarters, known locally as North Avenue.

To protect our anonymous sources, we give them pseudonyms. We referred to this particular source as *McDonalds*. In emails, conversations, text messages—everything. The source is always *McDonalds*. Our initial meeting, in 2017, took place in a McDonald's parking lot. If this source were ever discovered by North Avenue, they would certainly be investigated and likely fired. To ensure their protection, I'm the only member of Project Baltimore who knows *McDonalds'* actual name. We also limit the use of gender pronouns to further conceal identities.

McDonalds offered me report cards that were printed before and after grades were changed. The initial report cards showed 13 students failing a total of 18 classes. The timestamps told us the first versions were printed on November 11th, six days after the quarter ended, and final grades were submitted.

Nineteen days later, on November 30th, the report cards were printed again. And we could see that every single failing grade was changed to 60, the lowest passing score. In some cases, the course names weren't even re-entered. Comments, meant to alert parents of their children's poor performance, were deleted. *McDonalds* said no extra work was turned in by the students and no extra credit was given. The grades were simply changed so the students could pass.

As we dug deeper into the report cards, we found students who were absent or late to school nearly 40 days in just one quarter. Each quarter has about 45 days. Two of these students failed six courses total; every F was changed to 60.

"This is hard to believe," I said to *McDonalds*, as I looked over the report cards. I was truly stunned.

"It's common," *McDonalds* replied. "It happens at most schools."

Standing in that McDonald's parking lot, at that moment, looking at those documents, I realized we had embarked on a massive story. But I had no idea how big it would get.

"Why would someone do this?" I asked sincerely. The answer would forever change my perception of public education and lay the long-term foundation for Project Baltimore.

"You have to look at education from the standpoint of winners and losers," *McDonalds* explained. "Who benefits when more students pass?"

I didn't answer.

"If more students pass, the data of the school looks better. You need to understand, public education is not about students. It's about data. Every school is told to improve the data."

Looking back, I'm a bit embarrassed at my naivete. "Can't they just help the student—offer them tutoring?"

McDonalds flat out laughed. "That takes work. Changing a grade is easy. And the student moves on. He may not be able to read, but he's no longer your problem."

I saw one potential flaw in *McDonalds'* answer—state test scores.

Calverton Elementary/Middle, where that text and the report cards came from, was a school that struggled academically. According to state testing data, just two percent of Calverton students were proficient in English. One percent were proficient in Math. Let that sink in. ONE

PERCENT of the students in the entire school were proficient in math in 2017. That means 99% of the students were not proficient in math. And 98% were not proficient in English.

I challenged *McDonalds*. "Calverton's state test scores are terrible. You're telling me they're fixed?"

McDonalds head shook. "We don't have access to the state's computer system. We can't fix state testing. So, schools fix what they can."

We shared a few moments of silence as I processed what I'd just heard. I thought back to our interview with the Calverton teacher and Gregory Gray. Maybe it seemed too simple. Maybe I just didn't want to believe it. But their stories were simply real-life examples of *McDonalds'* claim.

Being honest, I didn't want to believe *McDonalds*. I'm a product of America's public school system. I wanted to believe that public schools are about the students. But I was just told it's really about the adults.

"As you do these reports, just remember," *McDonalds* explained before stepping into a car, "*everything* is about data. And data is money."

* * *

The documents and testimony we collected concerning Calverton contained extremely powerful allegations. Now, we needed an explanation. When we originally reached out to Calverton's principal, she directed us to North Avenue. Edie sent us this reply: "We received your email regarding the text. An investigation is currently underway with respect to grade-changing allegations at Calverton."

That answer was not good enough, which is why we went to the school in the fall of 2017. We wanted to get answers for students, parents, and taxpayers. What we got was the police called on us.

After I got off the phone with Edie, my photographer and I returned to the sidewalk on the Calverton side of the street.

"What now?" my photographer asked. His camera never stopped recording.

I looked around. The street was still lined with nice cars. "Give it a minute. Something will happen, soon." Inside that building, pressure had to be mounting on Principal Cooper to do something. Her employees surely wanted to go home. And they didn't want to be on TV walking to their cars.

After a few minutes, I heard my photographer grunt and gesture to the left. A marked police SUV was approaching. Once it slowed to a stop, a different officer stepped out of the vehicle. Simultaneously, the school door swung open, and the original officer reappeared.

In 2017, Baltimore City Schools employed just 100 police officers. Two of them were now approaching me. Both were armed.

"How you doing, bud?" The second officer asked.

"Doing well," I replied with respect.

He hastened his approach. This officer was many years older than the first and of a higher rank. He drove a white Jeep Liberty and wore a fancy hat with blue stripes across the bottom.

"Doing a good story?" He asked.

I folded my hands at my waist. "Trying to get a story. We're trying to speak with the principal of the school. We'd like to ask her about allegations of grade changing at the school. I only need a few minutes of her time."

The original officer was now standing off to my right. My photographer had backed off to widen his shot.

I continued to make my case. "We're not here to cause a problem. We don't want to make a scene. We just want to ask the principal a few questions about a text she recently sent to a teacher, and I also have some report cards I'd like to show her."

The officers had no interest.

"If she calls the police to have you removed, that's her way of telling you she don't want to speak," the first officer explained.

There it was. *That* was the soundbite I needed. It was short, but it said a lot. "She" called the police to have a reporter "removed" from a sidewalk because she didn't want to answer any questions. I looked at my photographer and nodded.

On the drive back to the office, as always, I gazed out the window at the miles of passing decay. I started to process what had just happened: two taxpayer-funded police officers kicked me off taxpayer-funded property so I couldn't question a taxpayer-funded principal about how she runs her taxpayer-funded school, where one percent of future taxpayers were proficient in math and two percent proficient in English.

Welcome to Baltimore.

C H A P T E R   2

"I BLAME THEM"

Our investigation into grade changing in City Schools clearly had some critics. In the early days of our initial coverage in 2017, we received plenty of voice messages and emails from disgruntled viewers. But we heard from many more viewers who supported our reporting and wanted to be included. Some parents were so upset with the school system, they would call Fox45 and demand to be interviewed. By the end of 2017, my desk began to stack up with report cards, progress reports, and transcripts showing grades were being changed all around the city. Most of the documents were sent by parents who only wanted one thing—a decent education for their kids.

I was stunned at how quickly viewers embraced the topic, both good and bad. We certainly struck a communal nerve. And this may be why.

In the early 2000s, when the rise of the internet threatened the budgets of local news organizations, the idea of a "beat reporter" began to fade. A growing number of television stations and newspapers around the country consolidated resources by staffing journalists who covered multiple topics. The traditional education beat reporters (a journalist who focuses on one "beat" or topic) began to vanish. Education reporting, while important, is often not considered a "sexy" news topic.

The watchdogs that once sat in every school board meeting were now covering murders, car shows, sporting events and blizzards. Many local government organizations, especially school boards, suddenly had fewer eyes on them. And parents had fewer media outlets willing to make their voices heard. At the same time, many places in America—including Maryland—were dumping billions of additional dollars into public education to meet the demand for improved student outcomes. More money, less oversight. What could go wrong?

Something else of significance happened when local beat reporting began to vanish: the media lost many of its experts. When a reporter focuses on one beat, they become an expert on that beat. Oftentimes, a beat reporter knows the subject matter better than the industry professionals they cover. But when you're not covering that beat every day, you miss things.

If school systems begin to subtly manipulate their data to make the district look better on paper, it could easily go unnoticed and therefore unreported. Next thing you know, as *McDonalds* said, nearly every school is changing grades. As a result, more students pass. Fewer students drop out. The graduation rates increase. School leaders gain recognition and larger salaries.

For the first 10 years of my career (2002–2012), I was a "general assignment reporter." All of my colleagues were general assignment reporters. We covered the news of the day. I could be in a jail, a farm field, a fire truck, a bounce house or a courthouse. It was fun; I learned a lot. But I could never dig into any one issue.

Beat reporting, in recent years, has started to make a comeback. To survive in a hyper-competitive environment, news outlets must produce compelling content, especially online. That is Project Baltimore. We are a team of beat reporters, producers and photographers. And when the public realized that, they responded. There was clearly an education reporting void in Maryland. People were frustrated, even angry.

By the fall of 2017, forty to fifty people a week were contacting us directly. Many of them feared their kids were being pushed through the school system without receiving the education they needed to support themselves or their families. They wanted their stories heard.

Of course, digging this deeply into billion-dollar issues, while being in the public eye, has its drawbacks. Claims of hatred and physical threats occasionally filtered through. Twice in 2017, once in 2018, and once in 2019, we had to call the police when targeted threats towards me went a little too far.

It's been a few years now since I received a significant threat. And it's not because we're doing anything differently. I truly feel this illustrates another benefit of beat reporting. When the community sees local journalists continually devoted to a societal issue, it earns respect and understanding. Plus, we were exposing major problems in Baltimore's public education system.

Here are a few headlines from Project Baltimore investigations over just one year, from July 2021 to July 2022.

July 14, 2021: *Baltimore City Schools: 41% of high school students earn below 1.0 GPA*

February 2, 2022: *77% tested at Baltimore high school read at elementary level, some at kindergarten level*

March 23, 2022: *Number of chronically absent students in Baltimore jumps to nearly 50%*

May 2, 2022: *Baltimore City student misses first 140 school days, marked present and passes classes*

July 13, 2022: *Report finds Baltimore City students with grades as low as 54% passed classes*

To further illustrate my point, here are a few more headlines from Project Baltimore investigations the following year, from August 2022 to August 2023.

August 1, 2022: *City student misses 96 straight days of school; Report card shows fake grades, attendance*

Sept. 12, 2022: *'Nothing stops a bullet like a job' | Educator says Baltimore youth murders tied to schools*

Nov. 2, 2022: *Baltimore test scores hit 13-year low as civil rights leader calls for CEO to be replaced*

Dec. 19, 2022: *Mom attends class with diabetic son despite City schools getting $32M to help hire nurses*

June 5, 2023: *Maryland NAACP calls education of Black students 'dreadful', warns school leaders*

* * *

Here's another example. The following story received a significant amount of feedback from viewers. It was a hard story to tell. But it was also powerful.

As we discussed, throughout the summer of 2017, we were in the process of collecting report cards and transcripts showing that grades were being improperly changed. Most of our evidence came from parents. Then, a high school teacher from Northwood Appold Community Academy II, or NACA II, contacted us. The teacher, who asked to remain anonymous, sent us a test that was given to seniors. Once we saw it, we were curious about what Baltimore residents thought of the questions.

We set up shop in Fells Point, which is a nice area of downtown Baltimore—shopping, restaurants, bars, fishing off the pier, etc. It's that type of area. We needed a large, diverse crowd. Fells Point provided that.

Around noon on a weekday, we placed a whiteboard on an easel and wrote out the questions from the test. We picked a busy street corner and started asking people to take the test.

Some of the test takers thought it was a trick. Others weren't sure what to think. But when they were finished, almost everyone had the same reaction.

Here are the questions that appeared on the whiteboard. These questions were written exactly as they appeared on the test.

"Draw a question mark."
"Draw a period."
"Draw an exclamation point."
"True or false, the defect in a program is called a bug."
"What is the acronym for Random Access Memory?"

A first grader who took the test got two correct. A fourth grader got all of them correct.

We asked participants to guess which grade level in City Schools received this test. Some people said first grade. Some said fourth or fifth. The highest grade we heard was ninth. When we explained this was part of a final exam given to seniors in Baltimore, everyone was stunned.

"That's pretty appalling," replied one lady.

"I think it's a justice problem that reflects a broken system," said a second woman. "It makes me sad about our school system."

"I think the school system is failing someone if they can't answer this question," added a father as he held his young son.

One man expressed this thought, "So, they're pushing the graduation numbers by lowering the bar."

Our goal was not to embarrass city students. But rather inform the public of the standards to which some students are being held. Once we had the public's reaction, our next step was to interview the teacher who gave the test.

"That test should be for an elementary school student," the teacher told me. We referred to this teacher as Yellow Flowers. In our interview with the teacher, we used a vase of yellow flowers to help conceal the person's identity. When I asked Yellow Flowers why that test was given to a senior, I received this reply. "Because that is the level they were functioning on."

Yellow Flowers perfectly fit the mold of a teacher who would contact the media, new to the profession, and had just taken a job in Baltimore. Yellow Flowers (I'm avoiding pronouns here) had no idea how far behind the students would be in their education.

As we worked to corroborate Yellow Flowers' story, we sought out other teachers at NACA II. I remember knocking on the door of an older gentleman who had been teaching in City Schools for decades. He couldn't understand why we thought the test was a story. To him, it was normal.

"A lot of the kids were not at grade level as far as being able to function and read accordingly," Yellow Flowers explained in our interview. "In order to survive in the classroom, as a teacher, it was easier to dummy it down. If there was work that was above the student's head, they would shut down. The system has failed our children, and we are allowing it to continue."

At this point in 2017, Project Baltimore was still relatively new. Similar to most government organizations, City Schools was used to general assignment reporters who occasionally appear for one report and then vanish for a while. So, when we asked for an interview to discuss the NACA II test, the district made available then Chief Academic Officer (CAO), Sean Conley.

Conley was a middle-aged career administrator. His answers reflected that—very scripted and robotic. The non-answer, answer kind of bureaucratic.

"Our work is aligned to the Maryland Career and College Readiness Standards. Point blank," Conley stated to start the interview.

I gave him some time to run through all his rhetoric. Then, with the cameras rolling, I handed him the test.

After allowing him a few moments to review it, I pointed at the test, "Does that seem to meet the standard?"

Conley never looked at me. His eyes were fixated on the test. And his body language did not match his dismissive words. "I would have to look into this and look at each of the questions to see if it would meet the standard."

The CAO refused to give an opinion. I could tell he wanted out of this interview.

"You don't have a first impression?" I asked.

Conley responded, "I don't like to assume or jump to conclusions. But it is definitely something I would want to look at."

That interview was one of the final interviews City Schools would grant Project Baltimore. Conley did not look good. When the story aired, viewers watched their Chief Academic Officer (who made $180,000 that year) look at the questions on the test, and then say he needed to look at the questions on the test before commenting.

This report hit the audience hard. The comments online varied greatly. Some people were critical of the school for failing to properly educate the students. Some people were critical of the teacher for leaking the test to the media. And some people were critical of Project Baltimore for reporting on the test.

But that test wasn't all we had from NACA II. During our investigation into the school, we also obtained final grades, as submitted by a teacher, and report cards. Here's some of what we found that we included in a separate report. One student failed physics and a foreign language his senior year, both required courses, yet that student walked across the stage during graduation. Another student graduated after being absent or late to school more than 100 days during the year, and had a first-quarter GPA of 0.000. We found six seniors who failed Spanish II, another required class, yet everyone graduated.

In the world of public education, graduation rates are possibly the most important data of all. In 2017, NACA II, where the test came from, had ZERO students score proficient in state math testing and five percent score proficient in English. Statewide, that same year, 36 percent of students were proficient in math, 44 percent in English. Yet, NACA II and the state both recorded the same graduation rate of 87%.

Does that make sense to you?

* * *

As mentioned, towards the end of 2017, Project Baltimore was being overwhelmed with calls, messages and emails from parents concerned about the negative impact of grade changing. One message was left by a woman named Michelle Bradley. Bradley had two daughters in City Schools. But when she called our tipline, her message was not about her children.

"Are you sure you want to go on camera?" I remember asking when we first spoke on the phone.

I knew telling a story like Bradley's would not be easy. We would certainly receive pushback. But people needed to hear it.

Bradley lived in one of the oldest low-income housing developments in the city. At least, that's what I assumed from its condition.

We pulled into the community around 11:00 in the morning. The parking lot was full. But no one was outside. It was a bit eerie. The community expanded over multiple city blocks. It was your typical brick government construction where everything looks the same—tiny porches, small windows, no landscaping.

Bradley lived on the second floor of an end unit. The trek to her apartment was short but challenging. The walkways were mostly hidden under broken glass, needles, and beer cans. The door leading to her home was locked. But judging by the looks of it, a light push would have snapped the hinges.

The doorbell didn't work, but the heat sure did. Outside, it was probably 25 degrees. Inside, her apartment had to be 90. As my photographer was setting up the lights and tripods, I could see the heat was affecting him. He was dressed in heavy winter clothing and setting up heavy equipment. But he was too polite to say anything. So, I tried to help.

"Ms. Bradley," I said. She was sitting hunched over the edge of a small dining room table. A larger woman with short hair, she patiently waited in silence. Bradley worked overnights cleaning houses. She was still in her work clothes when we arrived. "I hate to ask you this, but can you please turn down the heat? If you tell me where it is, I can turn it down."

There are no words to describe the look of pity that wrapped her eyes. I regretted asking the question before she replied. Bradley slowly drew in some hot air and said in the sweetest possible way, "Honey, this is the projects. We don't control our heat."

This is a woman whose frameless family pictures were resting on a shelf of unfinished two-by-fours. The stairs leading to her apartment were missing entire steps. Much of her vinyl flooring had peeled up, exposing the plywood underneath. I saw no food in her kitchen or paper towels. And I had the gall to ask her to turn the heat down because my photographer and I were uncomfortable. I can't ever remember feeling so small.

Then, what she said next, hurt even more. "We can't open our windows, either. They don't let us."

I just looked at her, ashamed. I was so disappointed in myself. I wanted to say, I'm sorry. But I couldn't bring myself to do it.

"At least, we're not cold." She added in her soft voice, while staring down at the table.

A few minutes later, my photographer finished his setup. He set the record, and we began.

We started the interview by discussing Bradley's two daughters. They were sitting with her at the table, though not included in the shot. Within her children's education, Bradley found the joy and pride she had been missing for most of her life.

"I'm very, very proud," she wept, speaking of the two high schoolers. "Very proud." She paused to wipe her tears. "What makes me so happy is that I kept my child. And my child . . . she can write. She's a good reader. She's a good reader."

Bradley grew up in Baltimore in the 1990s. She explained to us that halfway through middle school, she began to struggle. Her mom was on drugs. Her father was dead. If she went to class, she acted out and fell behind. But she says she kept passing. Every year, she explained, she continued to progress to the next grade for one reason.

"They kept saying I was getting too tall for the school that I was in."

Too tall for middle school and pushed into high school. Bradley, who is around six feet tall, was now in high school, where she simply couldn't do the work.

"No one wanted to help me." She spoke so softly, I strained to hear. "I couldn't get help. So, I just got frustrated and dropped out. I know it's easy to judge me. But until you walk a mile in my shoes," she paused. "It's very embarrassing."

Since leaving school in ninth grade, Bradley told me how she's been teased and mocked. Jobs have been hard to get. If she did get work, she says employers would take advantage of her when they realized she couldn't read.

She told me about a housekeeping job she had where she would work eight hours and only get a paycheck for $40.

"My supervisor picked up on that I could hardly read, and for a long time, he had cheated me. I was only bringing home $40."

And she didn't know.

When I asked her how she survived, she broke down in tears, "It was hard. It was hard. It was very, very hard." She looked up, dabbing her eyes. "They failed me because if you're passing me but you know I'm not getting this, then yes—I blame them."

Remember, Michelle made it to ninth grade in Baltimore City Schools.

"I joke a lot to cover up for hurt and pain. Because I couldn't hardly read, they would laugh. She can't hardly speak, she's stupid. She's dumb. When you stutter, you get teased. But when you can't read, you feel like a fish out of water."

She told me she stayed in her situation because she was afraid. "I had grown adults tell me you're not going to be nothing. And I believe it."

Bradley called Project Baltimore because she watched our reports on grade changing. She wanted people to know the long-term impacts it can have on a life.

"This is embarrassing, but if my testimony can help somebody, help a child, that is like me, I'll take the laughs. I'll take all of it. I hope, number one, that no child goes through what I went through. I hope they will pay attention to the kids in the school system. Don't just pass the kids through. If you know they can't read or comprehend, if you can help them, help them."

At age 39, Bradley was diagnosed with dyslexia. The school system, she says, never caught it—or never cared to try. Michelle's two daughters read to her. They help their mom read her mail and fill out job applications or medical forms.

"I would love to one day be a homeowner. I'd love to provide more for my kids and move them out of this neighborhood," she stated, as if it were only a dream.

After the interview was over, we needed some more video for our story. We got some emotional shots of Michelle laughing with her daughters at the table.

"Are you good?" I asked my photographer, referencing our video.

He shook his head. "I need more."

I looked around her cramped apartment. There were no other good visual options.

"Michelle," I asked, "would it be possible to go outside, and get some video of you walking around with your daughters? We just need a little more video."

She turned towards the front window. It was now about 12:30 in the afternoon and people had begun to gather outside.

"No," she stated. "It's safer in here."

* * *

Bradley's call to Project Baltimore came at a crucial time. We were about five months into our grade-changing investigation. With NACA and Calverton, we now had two schools where documents, confirmed by staff interviews, appeared to show that grades were being improperly changed. We had testimony from parents, *McDonalds*, Yellow Flowers and other teachers. City Schools announced it launched internal investigations into grade changing at both schools. Now, it was time to see how widespread the issue really was.

In the fall of 2017, I filed two public records requests with Baltimore City Schools for emails, internal investigations, and documentation related to grade changing. I asked for all documents going back three years. A few weeks later, we received a reply. We expected to get some documents. But the school system denied our entire request. They gave us nothing. Not one page. Not one word.

The district backed us into a corner. The day we received that denial letter, we gathered as a team. If we wanted the documents, there was only one way to get them. We took a few weeks to find the right attorney. Then, in December 2017, we sent a shockwave through the state of Maryland by suing Baltimore City Public Schools.

CHAPTER 3

"PRETTY OBNOXIOUS"

"What are your thoughts?" I asked our attorney as we walked into the courthouse.

Behind him, on a dolly, he pulled four boxes of case documents. "I think it's incredible that we had to go this far."

When we filed the public records lawsuit against Baltimore City Schools in December 2017, I didn't think it would last long. In our view, City Schools had clearly violated public records law by not releasing any records after we requested them. But in the face of a legal challenge, City Schools didn't back down; it doubled down.

In the months that followed the lawsuit, the district acknowledged its legal error and began releasing some documents. But the records we received weren't necessarily relevant to what we requested. Many documents appeared randomly selected with partial redactions that weren't clearly explained. Every few weeks, we'd get some more documents that didn't relate to grade changing. After each small records dump, City Schools would wait for our reply. Each time, we'd reiterate our demand for everything we originally requested—every email, document and internal investigation related to grade changing.

I got the feeling the district was releasing small amounts at a time, hoping we'd be satisfied and drop the suit. I also got the feeling they were releasing random documents just to tell the court they were honoring the spirit of our public records request. To me, it felt like they were playing a game, a very expensive game.

This absurd back-and-forth continued until our first court date in August 2018. During the hearing, a judge heard just a few hours of testimony. Before dismissing for the day, the court ordered City Schools to release additional records that must be pursuant to our original request. And they did. A couple of months later, we received 106 documents related to grade changing. We televised what each page looked like.

Following a public records request into allegations of grade changing in City Schools, this is what we received: 106 completely redacted pages.

That's 106 pages of black, completely redacted. Apparently, within those 106 pages, there was not one word, not one letter, that City Schools felt the public had the right to read.

"Almost a year to get. And this is what you got?" laughed Lucy Dalglish, the Dean of Journalism at the University of Maryland. Dalglish is an expert in public records policy. "This is kind of a poke in the eye. Kind of pretty obnoxious."

We interviewed Dalglish at her campus office. Her expertise was extremely valuable in our understanding of the situation. This was the first time in my career that I was involved in a public records lawsuit. It's common for government organizations to block the release of information.

But it's not common for media organizations to file lawsuits. It's expensive. And you're not guaranteed a victory.

Public records laws are tricky. They are different in every state in terms of enforcement and scope. Some states take open records laws seriously. Some don't. Maryland is somewhere in the middle. I've worked as a journalist in six jurisdictions—Wyoming, Wisconsin, Pennsylvania, Virginia, Maryland, and Washington, D.C. In my travels, I've noticed that while laws are different, government agencies often act the same. They don't like transparency. They don't want transparency. They just want your money.

Many government organizations use public dollars to hire lawyers to find legal loopholes to prevent public documents from being released to the public.

They will delay responding to a request in the hopes you forget about it. They will charge outrageous fees that they know you won't pay. I've had schools drag out the release of documents, hoping by the time I get them, the "news" is too old. The bureaucratic machine has all sorts of tactics to protect itself from oversight. Essentially, in my experience as a journalist, your government doesn't want you to know what it's doing.

In most states, public records laws don't have the teeth to sufficiently punish the bureaucrats who violate those laws. Think of it this way: the government wrote the laws that hold the government accountable. When the public or members of the media run up against an agency that simply refuses to release information, the only real option is to file a lawsuit. In our case, even after we sued, Baltimore City Schools still didn't seem to take the situation seriously.

"Maryland requires that you show bad faith. And quite honestly, I don't think I've ever seen bad faith more obvious. This is Exhibit A," stated Dalglish, as she paged through the 106 completely redacted pages. "I guess it's back to paying more taxpayer dollars for lawyers at the state to defend against this lawsuit, which is really too bad. I imagine there are better things the school district could be doing with its money."

* * *

Dalglish was absolutely correct. Baltimore City Public Schools had better things to do with its money than fight us in court.

When I moved to Baltimore from Washington, D.C. in early 2017, I didn't know anyone. Yet, I was expected to turn investigative content immediately. So, I did what investigative reporters do: I started analyzing data.

I pulled the state test scores for all roughly 160 elementary, middle and high schools in the city. I had no idea what I would find. But I felt test scores were a good place to start. The data sets for state testing results were massive and not well organized. It was just thousands and thousands of data points (test scores) on a spreadsheet. The data was not analyzed or grouped in any meaningful way. It was just there.

By hand, I entered the information into Excel Spreadsheets so it could be organized. It took me 40 hours—one full week. It was brutally tedious. But when it was finished, I could compare every school in the city. I could see how each school did by grade and subject. I could see how many students took the state tests and how many scored proficient. And once I had all the numbers in one place, what we found was shocking. And the report that this data generated became Project Baltimore's first viral story.

Here is what we found: there were six schools in Baltimore City that did not have a single student proficient in any state-tested subjects. NOT. ONE. KID.

This was in 2017. At the time, City Schools received about $16,000 per student every year, which was the fourth highest in the country according to the U.S. Census list of America's 100 largest school systems.

When we put this story together, we interviewed a senior at Frederick Douglass High School in Northeast Baltimore. His name was Navon Warren. We met him one day towards the end of the year. As he walked out of Frederick Douglass after class, my photographer and I were waiting. We mic'd him up on the curb and went for a walk through the city.

The moment I met Navon, I knew he was a good kid. No taller than 5'8". No heavier than 140. He presented himself well and walked with confidence. You could tell he was ready to leave Baltimore. And he had worked hard to position himself for that. I admired Navon. But it was a struggle to get him to talk for the camera.

"You've been making this walk for four years?" I asked. We crossed the street towards the bus stop. In Baltimore City, many students take public transit to school.

"Yes," was all he said.

"You ready to be done with it?"

"Yes."

I tried to follow up. "Move on?"

"Yes."

The bus had appeared from behind the hill, "Then what?"

"College." The bus stopped. The door opened. He stepped on.

Thankfully, Navon's mom, Janel Nelson, was far more talkative.

"I'm excited," she sighed in excitement. "It's been a long journey. This is a difficult city to be in. Very difficult city to be in."

Every day, when Navon walked home, he passed through an unforgiving city, abandoned homes and faded memorials. But this teenager bore his own scars.

"All the males in my family were killed," he told me, with little passion in his voice. I got the feeling, over time, that he numbed the pain by numbing his emotions.

At three months old, Navon lost his father in a shooting. Before his 18th birthday, he would lose two uncles and a close high school friend. That's four male figures in his life, murdered. All before he could legally vote.

"I've lost a lot of people, so I'm used to it. It hurts." Navon spoke quietly, eyes down, monotone. "I just choose not to show it. I just keep it in. You just have to live on and keep going on every day. You have to do it somehow."

His mom responded, "My motto in my house is: failure is not an option. I wasn't going to allow him to fail."

We spoke to Navon because he attended one of the six schools that had zero students proficient in any state testing.

"That's absurd to me," replied Janel, when we told her no one in her son's school scored proficient in state testing. "I don't understand how in an entire school not one person can be proficient."

The list of city schools, in 2017, with zero students proficient included five high schools and one middle school.

Middle School:

Booker T. Washington Middle School

High Schools:
Frederick Douglass High School
Achievement Academy @ Harbor City
New Era Academy
Excel Academy @ Francis M. Wood High
New Hope Academy

Here's how the assessment process worked in 2017. Students were tested by the state in math and English. Their scores place them in one of five categories. A four or five is considered proficient; one through three are not. At Frederick Douglass, in 2017, 185 students took the state math test. Eighty-nine percent fell into the lowest level. Just one student approached expectations and scored a three. In other words, only one student was even close to scoring proficient.

1: Have not met expectations – 89% (165 students)
2: Partially met expectations – 10.5% (19 students)
3: Approaches expectations – .5% (1 student)
4: Met expectations – 0%
5: Exceeded expectations – 0%

"That's your teacher's report card. Ultimately," Janel said. "How is it not one child passed? That makes no sense."

Navon was a young man who faced incredible adversity. His father and two uncles were murdered. He lived in one of the poorest neighborhoods in one of America's poorest cities. And he attended what could be Maryland's lowest-performing school. Yet, despite all of that, he found a way to succeed. He found hope in swimming. But he doesn't just swim. When we interviewed him in 2017, he was the reigning Baltimore City 50 and 100-meter freestyle champion who competed at the junior Olympics—and finished fourth. For Navon, the water is where the grit of the city is washed away. It's where he's untouchable. It's where his future is clear.

"I'm competitive," he told me. "I want to be number one."

That drive allowed Navon an opportunity to define his own future. In the fall of 2018, he told me he planned to leave the streets of Baltimore to attend college and swim.

"It's exciting for him to get out of the city and exciting for him to start a new chapter in his life," his mom told me.

"I took everything serious and tried to do my best every time," added Navon.

His mom looked over at him and smiled, "I'm proud of you."

In the years since we interviewed Navon, I have repeatedly tried to reconnect with him and his mother. I have not been able to reach them. I pray he is ok.

* * *

Navon told me he believes zero students scored proficient at Frederick Douglass, because the state tests are more advanced than what the students are learning. Based on that high school test from NACA II we discussed earlier, he may be right. So, we wanted to ask City Schools CEO Dr. Sonja Santelises. At the time, Dr. Santelises had been on the job for about a year. She declined an interview.

Dr. Santelises became Baltimore City Schools CEO on July 1, 2016— just about eight months before Project Baltimore launched. She was certainly qualified for the job. Universities such as Brown, Columbia and Harvard appear on her resume. She worked her way up through various school systems in Boston, New York and Baltimore. Before being named CEO in Baltimore, she served as the district's Chief Academic Officer.

I've had very few run-ins with Dr. Santelises. But people tell me she's very nice. I would like to build a professional relationship with her, but she avoids me. In fact, there's evidence she may really dislike me.

On August 22, 2024, Dr. Santelises agreed to a rare sit-down interview with local media (I was not one of them). She was asked by a *Baltimore Sun* reporter what her "biggest challenge" had been during her eight years as CEO. She answered, saying the hardest aspects of the job have been trying to improve math scores and attending the funerals of murdered students.

She then said this, "Baltimore City has been good to me. It has been good to my family. My husband has not punched out Chris Papst, which is great because I don't want him going to jail. We have college tuitions to pay."

The reporters in the room awkwardly laughed.

However, since she's talking about money, it's worth pointing out that in 2024, Dr. Santelises made $479,672 in total compensation. That includes her base salary ($349,989), cashing in unused paid time off (she gets nearly 12 weeks a year), "Deferred Compensation" towards retirement (which is in addition to her state pension) and a $9,600 car allowance.

Dr. Santelises is the highest-paid K-12 school leader in Maryland, overseeing a school system with around 75,000 students, 93% of whom are minority students. To put her earnings into perspective, the superintendent of New York City Public Schools oversees one million students and earns about the same amount.

It is common for the objects of investigations not to be fond of the investigators. After all, Project Baltimore has exposed many troubling and embarrassing scandals during Dr. Santelises' administration—reports that went viral. Many of them appear in this book. But are those reports my fault?

When we sued her district in 2017, that certainly soured our relationship pretty early on. And that relationship never recovered. Over the eight years this book covers, I've probably asked Dr. Santelises hundreds of times for an interview. She says no just about every time.

But think about it. Six schools with zero students proficient were not entirely her fault. However, it was her reality. But instead of confronting that reality, City Schools ran from it. They initially offered no one for an interview to add context to what we found in the data.

That changed after the story aired, probably because the report went viral. How could it not? The headline is stunning! It got picked up all over America and in other countries.

Headline: *6 Baltimore schools, no students proficient in state tests*

When City Schools decided to do an interview, they provided Janise Lane, the Executive Director of Teaching and Learning.

"Who's at fault?" I asked Lane to start the interview.

"I'm not really sure there's one person who's at fault," she responded.

I replied, "Is the school district at fault?"

Lane shook her head, "I wouldn't say the school district is at fault."

I followed, "The school district takes no responsibility for six schools with no kids proficient?"

"I'm not saying we have no responsibility in that," she replied. "I think it's a lot of things coming together at the same time."

Lane told Project Baltimore, the six schools are on their radar. They get extra resources along with increased teacher and principal training. An approach, she says, that can improve test scores. Except it didn't.

"It is not satisfying for any of us in City Schools to see the data and the numbers that look like that. It's an ongoing work effort to improve student achievement because that is our ultimate goal," she explained.

"It's stunning. It really is. But it's not surprising, unfortunately," responded former Baltimore City Council member, turned charter school CEO, Carl Stokes. "The kids aren't learning. They should evaluate the schools and decide if the school is not working, then they must close that school. Put those young people in schools that are working."

Lane pushed back on Stokes' thoughts, "It's not that easy because every school has its own make-up in their community and how things work. Our goal is not to shut schools down. Our goal is to support schools."

The headline stating there were six schools with zero students proficient in state testing in 2017 was just one of the many headlines we found in the spreadsheet I created. Here is another one:

Headline: *13 Baltimore City High Schools, zero students proficient in math*

The following report was published in late 2017. Here is the script as it aired. Throughout this book, I will occasionally post the actual scripts I wrote for certain reports Fox45 News aired. Each script begins with an anchor toss. This is where the anchor sits at the desk and introduces the story to viewers. From there, the camera either comes to me for additional information or it goes to a pre-produced and edited "package" that expands on the anchor's introduction. Once you read a few of these scripts, you'll get the idea.

This script is a small glimpse into my world and how I produce the reports that make up this book. Try to imagine watching a local newscast on TV while reading these scripts. That will help.

((START SCRIPT))

((ANCHOR 1))

Tonight, an alarming discovery coming out of City Schools. Our Project Baltimore team has found that one-third of High Schools in Baltimore last year didn't have any students proficient in math.

((ANCHOR 2))

Project Baltimore Lead Investigative Reporter Chris Papst joins us now. Chris, it took weeks to go through all the data, and the results are hard to believe.

((PAPST ON CAMERA))

This is stunning. Project Baltimore took a close look at 2017 state testing data and discovered that a third of all City High Schools had zero students proficient in math. None. But that's not all we found. Just beyond these troubling numbers, we found a bright spot. That is where we start.

((TAKE PACKAGE))

(Students Chanting in the auditorium)

Most every morning, at Baltimore Collegiate School for Boys, starts the same way.

(Students Chanting in the auditorium)

Jack Pannell: Founder of Baltimore Collegiate School for Boys "There's an urgency about the work we're doing."

An urgency born out of need.

Jack Pannell: Founder of Baltimore Collegiate School for Boys "Nine out of ten black boys in Baltimore City are not reading at grade level."

Chris Papst: *Nine out of ten?*

Pannell: "Nine out of ten typically are not reading at grade level."

That grim statistic led Jack Pannell to open this North Baltimore school three years ago. As the name implies, in these halls, there are no girls.

Jack Pannell: Founder of Baltimore Collegiate School for Boys "They tend to stay very focused on their studies."

The charter school also has no entrance exams. What it does have is a school day extended by one hour, a teaching staff that is 60 percent male and shorter class periods. All of it tailored to how boys learn.

Jack Pannell: Founder of Baltimore Collegiate School for Boys "We designed this school to make a fundamental difference in the lives of mostly black and brown boys in the city."

That design appears to be working. Since 2015, the number of Baltimore Collegiate's boys who scored proficient in state math tests has spiked by 60 percent.

2015 – 9%
2017 – 14.4%

Papst: *Are you happy with your numbers?*

Pannell: "No. I mean, we can do better."

(Chanting)

But Project Baltimore discovered that as this school is making progress, many other City Schools seem to be going nowhere.

We analyzed 2017 state test scores released this fall. We paged through 16,000 lines of data and uncovered this: of Baltimore City's thirty-nine high schools, thirteen had zero students proficient in math. Digging further, we found another six high schools where just a few students tested proficient. Add it up—in half the high schools in Baltimore City, 3,804 students took the state test, and fourteen of those students were proficient in math.

Chris Papst: Project Baltimore (standing outside North Avenue) "With eye-opening results like that, we reached out to North Avenue. We had some questions. But no one inside this building would sit down with us to answer them. Instead, we got a statement. Concerning our investigation, it said:

"These results underscore the urgency of the work we are now pursuing. We must do more to meet the needs of *all* our students."— Baltimore City Public Schools

That work, according to the statement, involves a new math curriculum, enhanced teacher development and expanded partnerships to provide opportunities for students.

"There is no simple answer that will close the achievement gap for Baltimore's students. Though we all want to see results quickly, the work is hard and will take time."—Baltimore City Public Schools

(Chanting)

At Pannell's school, results took just two years. With 440 students, his school is now at capacity. Another 300 are on the waiting list.

Jack Pannell: Founder of Baltimore Collegiate School for Boys "We believe we can change the narrative. We believe we can change history. We believe we can change the status quo if we keep doing what we're doing."

((END PACKAGE/PAPST ON CAMERA))

Keep in mind, with thirteen high schools that have zero students proficient in math, Baltimore City Schools spend nearly $16,000 per student, per year. The fourth most nationally (U.S. Census).

((END SCRIPT))

* * *

That story also went viral when it aired. And it really put into perspective the educational shortcomings of Baltimore City Public Schools. Many outside influences make education in the city difficult. Poverty. Violence. Trauma. The students who walk into the schools every day, in many instances, leave very difficult circumstances, like Navon. And those factors should be taken into account. But after we aired the stories about the six schools and thirteen high schools, we were contacted by a city teacher who said there's another reason City Schools is failing. And it's a reason no one wants to discuss.

As is standard, the teacher did not want to be identified, fearing retaliation. We agreed to disguise their face, voice and give as little identifying information as possible.

The teacher came to our Fox45 studios. We set up in a side room where no one would see them.

"Baltimore Schools are not failing kids," the teacher came out strong with an unequivocal charge. You could tell this educator was tired of taking the blame. "I almost feel like the school system is being bullied."

For the past twenty years, the educator has taught in elementary and middle school classrooms throughout the city. For months, the teacher watched Project Baltimore investigate City Schools and agreed that North Avenue has its issues. But when it comes to overall student performance, low test scores or high dropout rates, the educator said most of the blame is due to one thing.

"It's a lack of parenting. Where are the parents?" asked the educator. "These kids are coming to us battered and bruised and hungry and starving for attention. Before we can teach this great lesson we've prepared, we have to meet their hierarchy of needs. We have to feed them. Sometimes, it's cold outside, they don't have socks on. We have to find socks for them."

The teacher said teachers have become parents.

"Yes. I've taken children home. I've taken children to buy clothes. I've brought clothes to school. Toiletries, because they had such a terrible smell. That's neglect."

This Baltimore native told Fox45 that some kids haven't seen a parent in days. Others, while still in middle school, have already joined gangs in search of adult attention.

"The kids are in the streets, taking care of themselves, running their households. And we're expecting them to come to school, sit down and learn?"

"When parents are called for meetings, they don't show up," continued the teacher. "When parents are called for report card nights, they don't show up. A lot of the parents we see on report card nights are not the ones we want to see. Those are the ones whose kids are doing great."

This teacher, who's the same demographic as most of the students, had a strong message.

"I'm trying to wake people up. It's something we sweep under the rug. We know it's there. But we push it to the side. I grew up in this city. I love Baltimore. But I hate what I'm seeing now. And it's not getting any better. It seems like it's getting worse."

* * *

No matter the reason why entire schools had zero students score proficient in state testing, the school system took decisive action to correct the issue by scrubbing the data.

After we reported on the six schools and thirteen high schools, Baltimore City Schools changed the way it reported state test results. In 2017, the school system made public the total number of students who took the state test and the total number who scored in each proficiency level.

Starting in 2018, the school stopped posting total amounts for every school. Instead, if fewer than 5% of a school's students tested proficient, the district simply reported a vague statement saying, "less than five percent."

In other words, the data was hidden. We could no longer determine if a school had zero students who tested proficient. Ergo, no embarrassing media headlines.

Problem solved.

Except, a few years later, the state changed the annual standardized test that students took. Maryland went from PARCC to MCAP. When the test changed, so did the way the results were reported. And we could once again determine the number of students who scored proficient in each school. In 2023, we re-ran our data analysis.

Six years later, how many Baltimore City schools do you think had zero students test proficient in math? Here's the headline we ran on February 6, 2023.

Headline: *23 Baltimore schools have zero students proficient in math, per state test results*

Of those twenty-three schools, thirteen were high schools. At the time we produced that report, Baltimore City had thirty-two high schools. Meaning, in 40% of the high schools in Baltimore City, zero students tested proficient in math.

C H A P T E R 4

GETTING A PROMOTION

Baltimore City Schools is one of those school systems where many things don't seem right. When I first came to Baltimore, people spoke of widespread grade changing, increasing rates of student violence, inflated graduation numbers and so on. But most of it was anecdotal. When Fox45 News launched Project Baltimore in early 2017, viewers contacted us with stories, "They had heard." We received many emails that started, "You should look into this . . ." Essentially, much of the data surrounding the school system did not seem to match reality.

But once our investigative unit started producing meaningful, and quite frankly, shocking reports, the nature of our tips changed. The calls or emails no longer referenced rumors. We were hearing directly from the victims or witnesses. Gossip became reality, featuring those affected.

For example, how can students who miss more than 100 days of school a year, or fail ten classes in three years, still put on a cap and gown and walk across a stage during their high school graduation? That question is no longer a historical anecdote. We learned that the question was a reality at Joseph C. Briscoe Academy in West Baltimore.

We got on this story when a teacher at Briscoe contacted us. Like most teachers, she didn't want to be identified, fearing retaliation. She didn't want to be interviewed in any way—no silhouette, no anonymity, no anything. She just wanted to blow the whistle on what she saw as an injustice (I'm using pronouns because this teacher never went on camera).

For months, she prepared by collecting school records and student information. She gathered report cards, transcripts and attendance rates. When she felt she had enough evidence, she emailed it all to me and basically said, "Here you go." What she gave us didn't seem real. Our high-level sources within the school system confirmed the authenticity of the documents. But as we began putting a report together, something was missing.

We did everything journalists do when presented with sensitive information. We confirmed the documents were real. We triple-checked the data. We interviewed experts and reached out to the City Schools administration. We had everything to construct a powerful and consequential report that would grip the community. But we needed more. We decided we needed the students whose names appeared on the records.

This was not an easy decision for us. As journalists, we protect the identities of those who require protection. But, in this case, we felt the public needed to hear from the students whose transcripts we were reporting on. We always hear from the adults. We needed to hear from the people most impacted. So, we tracked down a former Briscoe student who had walked at graduation the year before. He was twenty years old and no longer enrolled at the school. We never used his name; we didn't want it to live forever on the internet. We just wanted his thoughts, and they were eye-opening.

The former student lived in West Baltimore. His neighborhood was very similar to the kind described in the opening paragraphs of this book, where windows are covered with plywood and the front stairs are sinking into the pavement. My cameraman was stationed behind me as we approached his home. Our producer was off to the left, recording with an iPhone. We had a graduation photo. So, I knew what the student looked like. When I knocked on the door, he answered.

"Hi (redacted name), my name is Chris Papst with Fox45 News," I began. "We are doing a story on Joseph C. Briscoe Academy. I have a microphone on and this is being recorded."

He was clearly surprised that I was standing at his door. But he didn't seem surprised regarding why. This former student looked to be your everyday kind of guy. But he had a crazy story to tell.

"We received your transcripts and your report cards from the school," I explained. "Can I ask you a few questions about your time there?"

Briscoe is a special needs school. It has just 79 students. With a budget of $4.3 million, the school at the time spent $54,524 per pupil. By comparison, Baltimore Polytechnic Institute, one of the city's leading high schools, spent $6,967 per student. Briscoe's mission is to educate students who require more attention than what an average Baltimore school would provide. But Briscoe's students are not unable to learn. Their need for additional attention generally stems from behavioral issues.

Before we hear from the student, it's important to add some context. For this report, we also interviewed a Briscoe teacher (not the one who gave us the documents) who explained how the at-risk nature of the student body demands a higher degree of expectation, not less.

"Yes," stated the teacher. "That should be the number one goal that they get the *right* education," this teacher strongly emphasized the word "right."

Fearing retaliation, this Briscoe teacher asked not to be identified, but told Fox45 that Briscoe is a troubled school. The year prior, 89 percent of its students were chronically absent. In 2017, Briscoe was one of the schools where not one student scored proficient in any state testing. Its four-year graduation rate is five percent. That is not a typo; the graduation rate is five percent. The city average hovers around 70 percent. Maryland's state average sits around 87 percent. The teacher we interviewed said the students at Briscoe need help.

I asked the teacher if failing grades were being improperly changed to passing at Briscoe.

"Correct. In my eyes, that's not really helping them because they're not prepared for what they're going to face in adulthood."

The previous school year, six students wore caps and gowns and participated in Briscoe's graduation ceremony. We obtained final grades and transcripts for two of them. One student was absent, or late, 110 days during his senior year. City Schools records show he failed science, a required class, with a 59. His transcript says he got a D-. He graduated in June.

The documents we had at Briscoe were very similar to the documents we had at NACA and Calverton. For each school, we had something unique. NACA had the test. Calverton had the text. Briscoe had a recording.

The recorded conversation was provided to Fox45. It came from inside the school shortly before the 2019 graduation. In it, you can hear what appears to be Briscoe administrators discussing a senior who failed.

The recorded conversation starts with a frustrated and loud female voice stating, "He couldn't have any work because he wasn't here."

A passive, perhaps scared, male voice in the room explained that the student being discussed never did extra work.

The following question was then asked by the female voice: "What can we do?"

Here's the response from different voices in the room: "So, we have to do a grade change? Is the final grade in there right now?"

"Yes."

After hearing the recording, I asked the teacher we interviewed if the referenced student deserved to graduate.

"No," was the reply.

This brings us back to the student we interviewed on that West Baltimore stoop. He failed ten classes in his final three years of school. Yet, he earned a certificate of program completion. Certificates are listed in Maryland law as a form of graduation that acts as an alternative to the traditional diploma. They don't count toward a school's graduation rates, but students can take part in the ceremony.

"I can say some people who graduated shouldn't have graduated," he admitted to me.

"They just told you that you were going to graduation?" I asked.

"Yes," he replied.

I was curious. "Did you do any extra work?"

"Kind of. Sort of." He snickered. "But not really."

According to state law, certificates of program completion are intended for students with disabilities who "cannot meet the requirements for a diploma." The word "cannot" being the operative word. But the student we interviewed told me he failed classes because he just didn't go to school.

I said to him, "We have attendance records showing you missed about 110 days your junior year. Is that accurate?"

He laughed, "That's about right, yeah."

I continued, "Out of 180? And you still feel like you deserved to graduate?"

"Not really," he smiled out the side of his mouth. "I understand what you're saying, but I'm actually happy. To be honest, I didn't think I was going to make it."

Not only did City Schools decline an interview with Fox45, North Avenue seemed less concerned about what we found and more concerned about how we found it, saying in a statement: "We understand the reporter has confidential student records and directly questioned the students. We are investigating how these records may have been received."

As for Briscoe's principal, Kamala Carnes, she also declined an interview. But we had questions. So, on a Friday morning before class started, my photographer and I went to the school and rang the doorbell. The visuals were similar to Calverton—red brick school, steel doors, a giant camera on a photographer's shoulder following a reporter holding a mic and a notepad.

"Hello." The voice came over the intercom after I pressed the button. The audio quality was terrible.

I leaned in to make sure they could hear me. "My name is Chris Papst from Fox45. I was wondering if your principal is available."

"Hold on, please."

For the next few minutes, nothing happened. My photographer and I just stood there—waiting. Then, I faintly heard a woman's voice opposite the blackened glass of the steel door. It seemed she was on the phone. So, I knocked.

"Are you Principal Carnes?" I was trying to see through the dark glass, but whoever tinted it did a really good job. "We just have a couple of questions. It will just take a minute of your time."

From the other side of the door, I heard a female voice yell, "No comment."

"You don't even know what my questions are. How can you say, 'no comment?'" I replied.

Thirty seconds later, that same voice asked that we leave school property. So, we set up shop on the sidewalk, about 150 feet from the door. A few minutes later, a school police officer arrived and walked inside. We waited for about two hours. No one came outside to speak with us. The district's PIO didn't even bother calling me. The school system, again, was not going to talk.

"These are special needs students," the Briscoe teacher explained to me. "The diploma is getting devalued. If they can't read and you're not giving them a type of trade or skill, and you're pushing them through the system, where will that leave them, once they graduate or get the certificate from the school, in life? How will they survive?"

Towards the end of our interview with the student, I asked him about his future plans. The 20-year-old said he didn't have a job. But he planned to eventually get one.

* * *

As you can imagine, the story of the former Briscoe student got a lot of attention. We ran it with the headline, "*Students Miss 100+ Days of School, Fail Classes, Still Walk at Graduation.*" The public's response on all our social media platforms was strong and diverse.

But one Facebook comment was worth paying closer attention to. As a side note, a "Bridge Project" was a secondary means of graduating for Maryland students. If a student could not pass the graduation exams offered by the state, students could opt out and, instead, complete a Bridge Project.

Facebook Comment from (name redacted):

"I worked here (Joseph C. Briscoe) when it was New Hope Academy. This isn't even half the story. I'd say more than half the students who graduated did so because they changed grades and/or falsified Bridge Projects. It's nice to see Briscoe continued the tradition of fraud when the city took the school back when our contract ended. They're all in on it. . . . And it's MUCH bigger than this one school. Charter and non-public schools in Baltimore are pretty much all scams. I actually quit the private special education company that staffed Briscoe because a) it had become far too dangerous, and b) they gave one of my students credits for a class she never even attended. Grade changing and fake Bridge Plans are almost a tradition in these schools. We used to joke that the person in charge of working with students on Bridge Plans had to graduate from city schools hundreds of times. Problem is, that joke isn't funny at all . . .

we graduated kids who couldn't read or write well enough to even fill out even the most basic job application. Right before I quit, I asked another employee about the grade change/fabrications for my students. She said, 'Our job is get them a diploma . . . she never would have gotten one on her own.' They would bribe kids to come in for one day during the summer ESY (extended school year) program, and then they would mark them present for the entire 4 weeks. It's all a scam."

Before our story aired on Joseph C. Briscoe, North Avenue declined an interview to discuss our findings. But two days after the story aired, City Schools CEO Dr. Sonja Santelises took to social media.

BALTIMORE CITY
PUBLIC SCHOOLS

Bernard C. "Jack" Young	Linda Chinnia	Dr. Sonja Brookins Santelises
Mayor, City of Baltimore	*Chair, Baltimore City Board of School Commissioners*	*Chief Executive Officer*

September 13, 2019

Dear Members of the Joseph C. Briscoe Academy Community,

I am writing to express our full support and deep concern regarding a negative story that aired on Fox 45 Wednesday night. Please know that I have every confidence in the dedication and professionalism of the staff and leadership at Joseph C. Briscoe Academy, as well as the leadership of Principal Kamala Carnes. I want our students and families to know that I am proud of their accomplishments and am filled with admiration for their resilience and determination. I want our staff and school leadership to know that I appreciate your willingness to accept the challenges that sometimes come with supporting students with special needs, and I applaud the empathy and understanding you bring to your jobs every day.

I want to make it clear that we have reviewed the records of students who graduated or received certificates from Joseph C. Briscoe last year, and all of them met the requirements for a diploma or a certificate of completion. I've also found no proof that any grades were improperly changed. Our students and families should be proud of their achievements, as are all of us at City Schools.

I am deeply concerned that Fox 45 has chosen to publicly undermine the efforts of our students in the interest of the station's sensationalism and ratings. I feel the reporter crossed a line by confronting students at their homes and directly questioning them, and I am appalled they used that footage. The reporter positions himself as an advocate for the community, but his stories are filled with inaccuracies and misleading statements. For example, the reporter did not make it clear that graduating with a high school diploma is different than completing a certificate.

We have consistently asked the Fox 45 reporter, managers, and owners not to share false information or invade families' privacy – but they continue to publish inaccurate information and show a lack of concern for our students and families. In this instance, there is no question that they violated even the lowest standards of decency and compassion for students and families who are most in need of our support.

We are also investigating the privacy law violations that have occurred. Staff, students, and parents have every right to speak with journalists and media outlets as part of their freedom of speech. But staff are bound by law and ethical values to protect our students' privacy.

I will keep you updated on any further developments on this issue, but do not hesitate to contact me if you have any questions or concerns. In the meantime, thank you for everything you do every day.

Sincerely,

Sonja B. Santelises

Sonja Brookins Santelises, Ed.D.
Chief Executive Officer
CitySchoolsCEO@bcps.k12.md.us

---

* * *

Let's dissect this letter, shall we?

Dr. Santelises came out strong, accusing Project Baltimore of "sensationalism" and "publicly undermining the efforts of students." She also opined that we "violated even the lowest standard of decency."

In the letter, Dr. Santelises expresses her "full support and deep concern regarding a negative story that aired on Fox45." She says she supports the leadership of Principal Kamala Carnes and was proud of the school's accomplishments. Keep in mind, this is a school with a 5% graduation rate, where 89 percent of the students are chronically absent. And in 2017, not one student scored proficient in any state testing.

The letter explains that North Avenue reviewed student records for the 2019 Briscoe class and found that "all of them met the requirements." Dr. Santelises says she was "appalled" that Project Baltimore was "confronting students at their homes." But contrary to the CEO's statement, the person we interviewed was not a City Schools student. He was a former student. A 20-year-old man, who wore a cap and gown the prior June. Plus, he wasn't confronted at his home. We knocked on the door and he spoke with us voluntarily.

While the letter says a lot, it doesn't mention the recorded conversation where school staff appear to be discussing a student's failing grade and suggest changing it.

"My first thought was, why? Why are they sending this letter? What's behind that?" Scott Marder was our attorney who sued City Schools for violating state public records laws. The Briscoe story aired while the lawsuit was ongoing. "Why are they now sending a letter that is factually inaccurate and broadcasting it to the whole school community?"

One factually inaccurate part was this: when Dr. Santelises attempted to discredit our reporting, she said Project Baltimore didn't make it clear that graduating with a diploma is different than a certificate of program completion. But the exact line from our story reads, "Certificates are for students with significant disabilities who cannot meet the requirements for a diploma."

This letter was a big deal. The highest-paid school CEO in the state was calling out a news station. When we responded by asking her to sit down for an interview, we couldn't even get a response. Time and time again, I emailed the school. I called the communications office. Nothing.

Either way, despite how City Schools felt about our reporting, the district did open an internal investigation into improper grade changing at Briscoe, just like it did following our reporting on Calverton and NACA II.

UPDATE:

The Briscoe investigation took eighteen months. Of the twenty-one teachers at the school, the investigator interviewed six. The teacher who gave us the student transcripts was not interviewed by the investigator. A second teacher we interviewed for the on-air story was also not interviewed by North Avenue's investigator. The recording we obtained of the school employees discussing changing the grade of a failed student was not addressed in the report.

The conclusion: When asked if improper grade changing was happening at the school, the result was "inconclusive." When asked if the principal of Joseph C. Briscoe allowed improper grade changing, the result was "unsubstantiated."

After 18 months, we learned City Schools doesn't know if improper grade changing happened at Briscoe. But it does know the principal didn't allow it.

More importantly, perhaps, we learned students can legitimately graduate from Baltimore City Schools after missing more than 100 days of class in a single year.

Which is worse, changing a student's grades so they can graduate, or admitting that students can be absent 55 percent of the time and still graduate?

* * *

One by one, we continued to profile additional schools that were accused, by their own employees, of changing grades. And we had produced dozens of other reports with parents, accusing their schools of doing the same. Pressure was mounting. School leaders were under a lot of fire. So much in fact, the president of the principals' union called me one day demanding I interview him. He didn't really have to demand an interview; I wanted to interview him. In fact, I had requested numerous interviews with him. He turned them all down. But now, all of a sudden, he was ready to speak. I suppose his membership was getting a little restless.

The principal's union is called the Baltimore City Public School Administrators and Supervisors Association—PSASA (pronounced: pah-zaz-zah). Their president at the time was Jimmy Gittings. Gittings is an older, African American gentleman. Softly spoken and frail, he's not the in-your-face hammer often associated with union presidents.

"Our principals are under a microscope right now," he told me, seated in front of his brick fireplace. He lived far north of the city, deep in the Maryland countryside. "The public and the news media, and I'm going to say you," he pointed at me, "you need to understand what these principals are going through."

For fifty years, Gittings was involved in Baltimore City Public Schools. First as a teacher, then as an administrator. And he admitted the pressure principals are under is the worst he's ever seen.

He continued, "That's why our principals might be doing things that upper management [or] the public might question."

Gittings explained how there's an intense pressure to raise test scores and attendance, which comes from North Avenue, specifically middle management. But he says that pressure to succeed does not always come with resources or guidance, leaving principals to do things "their way."

I pressed Gittings. "Leaving principals to do things their way?"

"You will not get me to publicly or privately say that our principals are doing something that is not right, let's put it that way," he replied. "Our principals are doing everything possible to ensure that our students are receiving the best education possible. And if they go about it in their way to make sure that a student receives the best education possible, it shouldn't be questioned. They should not be chastised or punished for it."

But Gittings says principals were being punished. He told Project Baltimore that, in the few months leading up to our interview in 2019, five principals had been removed from their schools. He wouldn't tell me why, but I had my suspicions.

Either way, I was still stuck on Gittings' statement that principals "shouldn't be questioned."

In Baltimore, principals earn healthy, large six-figure salaries. They get millions of dollars to operate their schools. And their union president says they "shouldn't be questioned?"

"I think it's ludicrous," he said. "Why remove a principal from a building. And you are investigating, the legal office is investigating alleged allegations that have not been proven at all, or substantiated?"

But even when allegations are substantiated, principals are not always removed. The union has a lot of power and influence, especially in Maryland. I brought up Calverton, the school where the principal sent a text to her teachers instructing them to change grades. Despite all the evidence against Calverton's principal, Martia Cooper, she remained at the school.

"She did and acted in a professional way, the way that she was directed to by middle management," Gittings added, speaking of Cooper. "I know you're going to take that comment out of context. She did what she was told to do."

My ears perked. "She was told to change grades?"

"No," he snapped. "She did what she had to do to ensure that the students at Calverton were treated in the respectful manner that they should have been treated in. The principal did what she had to do. That's as far as I will go with that."

"What does that mean?" I asked.

"That's as far as I will go with that." At this point in the interview, he shut down. We were done.

"The principal did what she had to do," he concluded.

* * *

Gittings was right. Principals are under immense pressure. The question is, what is that pressure intended to produce?

What you see below is from the Baltimore City Schools policy book concerning promotion, acceleration and retention. This is how it appeared on the district's website. The bolded sentence is bolded by City Schools, but it's not the most important sentence in this section.

---

c. Students identified for retention should be encouraged to attend an academic summer learning program as a method of supporting their continued learning.

d. Promotion considerations of students with disabilities are outlined in section II.

e. In grades K-8, a student may only be recommended by the principal for retention should a student meet the criteria outlined below. **All retentions must be approved by the principal's supervisor.** While students cannot be retained a second time prior to ninth grade, in exceptional cases, a principal may recommend to his/her supervisor additional retention(s) for approval.

This small section of the district's rule book contains what may be the most consequential regulation in the district. If your school system has similar language, it's likely greatly impacting your district as well.

Here is the important line: "Students cannot be retained a second time prior to ninth grade." What that language means is that a student cannot fail a grade more than once between kindergarten and high school. No matter how little work that student does. No matter how few times the student attends class. No matter the student's grades. No matter if the student understands the material or can even read, the student can only repeat a grade one time.

When parents and teachers say students are being pushed through the school system without getting the education they need, this rule is largely the reason why. If a student has already been held back in a grade, principals cannot hold them back again. Or, if a student should be held back in elementary school, a principal may choose not to hold them back and save the "one fail rule" for later years.

Early on in Project Baltimore, we interviewed a teacher (anonymously, of course) who told us this: "We have graduated kids who can't read. Illiterate. They had a diploma in their hands that they couldn't read. That sounds like an exaggeration or hyperbole. It's not."

It was hard to understand how that could happen until we learned about the "one fail rule." However, it doesn't apply to high school. In high school, students earn credits to graduate. But by ninth grade, many students have become accustomed to automatically being promoted. North Avenue has never granted us an interview to discuss this regulation. But they've defended it via statements.

> "The promotion and retention policy (Policy IKEA-RA) is based on academic research and was designed to make sure that students have the skills and opportunities to succeed. Students learn best with their grade-level peers, as has been proven consistently by data-driven research. As such, multiple retentions should be a last resort for students.
>
> We are committed to holding our students to the highest standards. It is our job to provide them with the supports they need to meet the rigorous standards so they can be successful in school and beyond.

There is a provision in Policy IKEA-RA that allows principals to request an exception, for extenuating circumstances. The exact language from the policy states: 'While students cannot be retained a second time prior to ninth grade, in exceptional cases, a principal may recommend to his/her supervisor additional retention(s) for approval.'"

What is more important to long-term success: a student demonstrating academic proficiencies before advancing grades, or promoting a student to maintain peer-level relationships?

* * *

In addition to the "one fail rule," City Schools also adopted what is often called "The 50% Rule."

Under Baltimore City Schools Board Policies, "The 50% Rule" says this:

c. <u>Failing Grades</u>: If a student receives an F as a marking period grade, the numerical equivalent of that grade cannot be lower than a 50 when used to calculate the student's final grade.

In other words, a student cannot earn less than a 50% as a final grade. The student could do nothing. They could never show up to class. They could turn in zero assignments or tests. Yet, that student will receive a grade of 50%.

Remember the name Diane Tirado? She was a teacher from Florida. In 2018, she wrote a whiteboard message for her class, which went viral.

The message said, "Bye, kids. Mrs. Tirado loves you and wishes you the best in life! I have been fired for refusing to give you a 50% for not handing anything in."

The school system says she was fired for poor performance. But Tirado claims she was fired for not following the school's guidelines that say a student cannot receive a grade lower than 50 percent. Both may be true.

"A grade in Miss Tirado's class is earned," Tirado said in a news interview at the time, "I'm so upset because we have a nation of kids that are expecting to get paid and live their life just for showing up, and it's not real."

"That's exactly correct," replied long-time Baltimore City Schools teacher Dana Casey. "They keep saying, let's just lower the bar and lower the bar and lower the bar a little bit more."

Concerning "The 50% Rule," North Avenue told Fox45, "The intent of the policy, and the longstanding practice that preceded it, is to ensure all students have an opportunity to improve performance throughout the year and can be motivated to overcome personal and academic obstacles to pass a course. If lower numerical grades for a marking period were permitted, a student could easily give up on a course when it became apparent partway through the year that passing was a mathematical impossibility."

"The emphasis is on passing," explained Casey. "The emphasis is not on learning. The emphasis on passing is important to North Avenue because it affects their numbers."

City Schools certainly has a reason to be concerned with its numbers. The National Assessment of Educational Progress (or NAEP) is a national standardized test. It's also known as The Nation's Report Card. Every couple of years, the federal government tests students in all fifty states and select cities to compare progress in subjects such as reading and math. Of the large districts tested, Baltimore is often America's second or third lowest performing, usually ahead of only Cleveland and Detroit. NAEP data (similar to state testing data) cannot be manipulated by local districts. Casey told Fox45, she believes North Avenue's 50 percent rule is a way to manipulate the data it can so that fewer students fail.

Casey stated that "the numbers look good. Look at all these kids passing. But they are in eighth grade, and they've got a second-grade reading level."

Outside Baltimore City, the higher-performing school systems of Anne Arundel and Howard County Public Schools do not have "The 50% Rule." But Baltimore County Public Schools does. It was adopted in 2016 as proficiency rates and standardized test scores began to drop.

Richard Wormeli is a former teacher turned education consultant. He travels the nation arguing in favor of the 50% rule.

"So, the question I would put forward to a teacher who was concerned about this is, do you give, or record, the most hurtful and unrecoverable end of the F range or the most hopeful and recoverable end of the F range, but nonetheless still an F?" Wormeli explained.

Wormeli says giving students a zero on a test or assignment may not accurately reflect how much they've learned.

"If we were to take temperature readings for a week, 85, 88, 87, 86 and so on, and we forgot to take the temperature on Friday. We might record nothing, which is, in essence, a zero. And if we had to average that, that would bring the temperature back down to the 60s, if we were reporting the temperature for that week. That would be a false report of what actually happened with the weather," he said.

"The 50% Rule," according to Wormeli, is a symptom of what he considers the real problem.

"We are so stuck on the hundred-point scale because it tends to be this: it was done to me, so it must be okay to do it to the next generation."

We need a new type of grading scale, believes Wormeli, with a smaller range, say 0-50, where if a student misses a test or is chronically absent, they can still pass a course if they can show they've learned the material.

Wormeli asked, "Did they (the student) present evidence of learning? That's what the grade is reporting. Not how hard they worked."

Casey completely disagrees.

"Once or twice on occasion it might help a kid here and there," she replied. "But it's ultimately destructive. They've sent out the message that you will not be held accountable, don't worry about it. I have seen over and over again that when you hold children accountable and set standards, they can rise to the occasion. And to constantly act like they are so crippled and broken that they can't learn, grow and push themselves, is repulsive to me."

In most school systems, including Baltimore City, a 60% is the minimum passing grade, a D-. If a student starts at 50%, it seems they only have to earn ten points, out of a possible 100, to pass a class.

* * *

There's also "Bridge Projects." We briefly hit on this in an earlier chapter. Going into the 2019 school year, City Schools' graduation rate was at a record high, with students from nearly every background and demographic earning more diplomas. That is great news. But when we dug deep into the numbers, we found there were questions about *how* those kids were graduating.

City Schools' graduation rate went from 65% in 2010 to about 71% in 2019 (the last full year before COVID). That's a significant jump. Now, here's the story behind those numbers.

In Maryland, in 2019, there were two ways a student could graduate from high school. The traditional way of earning credits and passing assessment tests, or with what is called the Bridge Plan. Starting in 2007, Bridge—according to the State Department of Education—was intended for students with disabilities, test anxiety and English Language Learners.

"Bridge Projects" were created for students who cannot pass senior exams in the various core subjects. "Bridge" is not a test, but rather an actual project that students complete in certain subjects to get a diploma. Our investigation found that Bridge had become very popular in City Schools.

In 2009, 20% of Baltimore City High School graduates used the Bridge Plan. In 2015, it jumped to 37%. By 2019, more than half, 50.4%, of students in Baltimore City were using Bridge Projects to graduate. In the Districts surrounding Baltimore City, that number was between 4% and 13%—the state average is around 10%. We found one school, Renaissance Academy, where 73% of its students were graduating through Bridge.

Baltimore City Students Graduating Via "Bridge Projects"

2009 – 20%
2015 – 37%
2019 – 50%

It's also worth mentioning that as Bridge graduates increased, the college enrollment decreased. In 2015, the college enrollment rate in City Schools was 44%. By 2020, it was down to 41%.

Ask yourself this: The "one fail rule." "The 50% rule." Bridge Projects. Who do those policies help more, the students who are passing grades and graduating in greater numbers, or the adults who run schools with better pass/fail data?

Remember what *McDonalds* said, "*everything* is about data. And data means money."

C H A P T E R   5

THE COVER-UP

Baltimore's court system does not work quickly. As Project Baltimore waited for our lawsuit against City Schools to progress through the courts, we continued to dig into other aspects of the district. And we learned it's not just grades being changed in an effort to improve school-level data.

When No Child Left Behind was signed into law in 2002, I was in college. President George Bush touted it as one of his great first-term achievements. Through media reports at the time, I gathered a basic understanding of its purpose. But when I started on the education beat, I gathered a deeper understanding of its consequences, good and bad.

I once interviewed a man who was running for the school board. He didn't win. But he said something during the interview that always stuck with me. And it turned out to be applicable to many circumstances. The man had been a Baltimore-area teacher for 33 years. Sixteen of those years were before No Child Left Behind and 17 years after. When the interview started, I asked him why he was running for the school board. He replied, "Because parents are being lied to." Following a few seconds of uncomfortable silence, he added, "The lie is that what we're doing is working."

He explained that during his career, he watched violence in the schools escalate. While at the same time, data collected by the state showed schools were much safer.

No Child Left Behind changed public education in many ways. One of the most significant changes came by way of encouraging the collection and analysis of a variety of data to determine a school's success.

Take suspension rates in Maryland as an example. In-school and out-of-school suspensions statewide plummeted 56 percent from 2007 to 2019 (the last full year before COVID). In Baltimore City Schools, the decrease was 62 percent. The school board candidate witnessed this reduction as a teacher. He told me students' behavior didn't change. The adults' response to that behavior changed. When schools report fewer suspensions, they appear safer.

In/Out Suspensions	Maryland	Baltimore City
2007	181,578	17,520
2019	79,306	6,665

But the state didn't stop there. Under Maryland law, if a school has too many suspensions, it can be labeled as "persistently dangerous." If that happens, the school can be placed on probation. Parents are notified. Students can transfer. Corrective plans are drafted. And school administrators could lose their jobs. Maryland has roughly 1400 public schools. As of 2021, zero were labeled "persistently dangerous." Not one school in the entire state. Now, why is that?

The board member said once a school gets close to being labelled as "persistently dangerous," school administrators will simply quit suspending students, no matter their actions. To a degree, that makes sense. In 2018, there was one school in Maryland on the "persistently dangerous" list, Friendship Academy in Baltimore City. The following year, the school was shut down. The message: Don't get on the list.

"One school I was at, the principal made a policy of not suspending students," the school board candidate told us. "He didn't broadcast that to the student body, but after a while, the students start to see. Well, so and so did this really bad behavior, and nothing happened to him. I'm gonna see what I can do."

He continued, "At one level, it sounds good for a school principal to say, 'We've had no suspensions at our school.' Implying that behavior is really good. Whereas, we know internally, the behavior is getting worse."

During the beginning of his career, the candidate remembers a student calling him a "stupid jerk." He says the kid was reprimanded, and his parents were called to the school. By the end of his 33-year career, he says, a student brought a knife to his class. The weapon was taken, but the student was not disciplined. The principal of the school did not want a record of a weapon being at his school.

The data requirements encouraged by No Child Left Behind can be beneficial. It made schools more transparent and more accountable. Journalists and the public now have access to massive amounts of school data, such as attendance rates, state testing proficiencies, suspensions, expulsions and so on. But when six-figure administrative jobs are tied to the data, how reliable is the data?

We interviewed one young lady who said the bullying and violence in her school got so bad, she transferred.

The student's name was Tone'yah Kemp. She was a sweet, young girl who loved to sing. Adele was her favorite. She sang "Hello" for us before the interview. The girl had talent. All she wanted to do was go to school and study music. But most days, she chose to stay home.

"I didn't want to go to school because they were on the steps, and it made me kind of sad. I started to spiral down into a depression," Tone'yah told me.

Tone'yah attended Lillie May Carroll Jackson Charter School in East Baltimore. All year, she says, a group of older girls every morning would block the steps, forcing her and other students to walk in the mud, snow or rain to get to class. If you're a middle school girl, this is a big deal. It prevented Tone'yah from wanting to go to school and enjoy what she loves—music.

"That's just sad because 6th graders and 5th graders have to walk in the mud just to get up to school. That's not cool," she said. Tone'yah would fake an illness or tell her mom she was too tired to go to school. But eventually, her mom learned the truth.

"They wouldn't allow them to pass." Crystal Kemp was Tone'yah's mom. "They would taunt them, call them names."

When the bullying didn't stop, Crystal called the school's administrator.

"They said, ma'am, this is an issue that's been going on all year. We are aware of it." Crystal grew visibly upset as she recalled the conversation.

"'Other parents have been calling about it.' She says, 'Well, we pulled the young ladies aside and we had a conversation.'"

But, Tone'yah says the conversation didn't stop the bullying. So Kemp began sending emails and filed a bullying complaint. She says the school responded by putting a sign on the steps. We never learned exactly what it said. But amazingly, it didn't work.

"I said, 'Why don't you discipline them? You can't suspend them? You can't send them home?'" asked Crystal, recalling her conversation with school officials. "They said we will not send the kids home. We will not suspend them because of this. So what do you do, just have a conversation?" Crystal's emotions trumped her ability to control them. She was flat-out enraged by the situation. Her daughter had no other choice. She changed schools. This young girl had to transfer because the administration would not stop a group of girls from bullying others.

So now, let's go back to the data. In 2007, the Maryland State Board of Education noticed that students of color and those with disabilities were being suspended disproportionately. So, the state pushed to reduce suspensions. As we discussed, it worked. They're down 56% over 12 years.

But as suspensions went down, reports of bullying went up. In 2018 alone, bullying reports filed in Maryland rose 33 percent (4,705 to 6,091). The number of reported incidents in Baltimore City was up 59 percent over the previous three years.

The same state data tells us that the most common corrective action schools took to address the problem was a student conference. Forty-three percent of the time, the school had a conversation with the bully. Thirty-four percent of the time, the bully simply got a warning.

As far as actual discipline, ten percent of bullying cases resulted in detention. Eight percent of bullies got out-of-school suspensions statewide.

Is there a connection between a rise in bullying complaints and a reduction in suspensions? Crystal thinks so. Now her daughter, who is a student of color, is a victim. Her daughter had to start over in a new school because the adults in her old school, she says, didn't address the issue.

Tone'yah left Lillie May. The last time we spoke with the family, Tone'yah was excited to take chorus in her new school.

No one from Lillie May would sit down with us for an interview when we did this story. We did receive a statement that read, "We strive for a school environment where trust, respect, responsibility, and joy in learning permeate the school culture. All reports of bullying are taken extremely seriously and investigated. Our school prides itself on approaching discipline in a way that promotes healing."

I wonder if that sign is still on the steps?

* * *

But it's not just suspension data that districts can actively minimize to make schools appear safer on paper. Here is a story we first aired in 2017, and then we did a follow-up five years later. This is how the script appeared as I wrote it in 2022. Again, try to read this and imagine a news report on your local TV station.

((START SCRIPT))

((ANCHOR))
An eye-opening Fox45 News investigation has found that the number of student arrests in Baltimore City Schools has plummeted **98 percent.**

((ANCHOR))
But as Project Baltimore's Chris Papst explains, the drop in arrests doesn't mean schools are safer. In fact, it could be making them more dangerous.

((TAKE PACKAGE))

((Police Siren))

Every year, for the past seven years, Baltimore has seen more than 300 murders. The city is fighting an epidemic of crime and violence, one not just confined to our streets.

City Schools Police Officers:

Chris Papst: "North Avenue does not want police officers talking to the media?"

Officer: "No. Because we know what's going on."

These whistleblowers asked not to be identified for fear of retaliation. But both say what's happening in the street is starting in the classroom, and city school police officers are not allowed to stop it.

City Schools Police officer: "Arrests are not being made when they need to be made. We are turning our heads on it."

((School fight video)))

We've seen the videos from inside City Schools, students fighting and teachers getting attacked. Project Baltimore has heard from parents worried that the violence has gotten out of control, making it difficult for other students to learn. Now, these two people who worked as school police officers tell us the reason it's gotten so bad is that they were not allowed to do their jobs.

Chris Papst: "City Schools is trying to keep arrest numbers down?"

Officer: "Yes."

Chris Papst: "Why?"

Officer: "Politics, sir."

In recent years, they say, school police officers have been pressured to reduce the number of arrests. From fights to more serious crimes involving weapons, assault, trespassing, and even burglary.

Chris Papst: "When you say burglarize, you mean they broke into a school?"

Officers: "Yes."

Chris Papst: "And stole things."

Officers: "Yes. Notebooks, Laptops, whatever they could find. Command staff said to detain them and release them to their parents. If you commit a crime, you go to jail. But instead of going to jail, we're doing paperwork to release them."

The number of students arrested in city schools has gone down significantly. Project Baltimore found that the number had plummeted by 98 percent over a decade. In the 2008 school year, nearly 1000 students were arrested. Ten years later, that number dropped to just 18.

Baltimore City School Police Arrest Trend Data

SY08/09 – 971
SY09/10 – 780
SY10/11 – 503
SY11/12 – 472
SY12/13 – 478
SY13/14 – 489
SY14/15 – 267
SY15/16 –   91
SY16/17 –   85
SY17/18 –   18

Source: Baltimore City Public School/Maryland State Department of Education

((File: 2017))

City School Police Chief Akil Hamm:
05:41 – "We're not where I want to be, but we're headed in that direction."

Baltimore City Schools declined an interview but said in a statement that City Schools implemented an intentional, multifaceted strategy that has resulted in fewer student arrests and has been held up as a national model.

In 2017, City Schools Chief of Police Akil Hamm spoke with Project Baltimore on this topic. Hamm said his department was no longer arresting students for what he considers low-level crimes.

City School Police Chief Akil Hamm:
5:51 – "We're not going to arrest all of the children. We're going to build positive relationships with kids, we're gonna nurture kids."

The intentions were seemingly good: create relationships between students and officers, encourage kids to ask for help, confide in police and stop problems before they occur.

City School Police Chief Akil Hamm:
10:00 – "To me, that's fruitful."

Chris Papst: Project Baltimore (stand-up)
"But did it make schools safer? When school police were told to stop arresting students for low-level offenses, were more serious crimes also overlooked? According to district data, in the 17/18 school year, which is the most recent data available, City Schools reported 3,734 instances of violence, including 81 for possession of a firearm or explosive, and 21 sexual assaults. Of those cases, only 202 were referred to law enforcement. We can't see what those 202 referrals were for, but we do know, only eighteen resulted in an arrest."

City School Police Officer:
"There is no such thing as a low-level crime when kids are hurting each other. If there is no discipline, the child is going to do it over and over again because they haven't learned anything."

These whistleblowers say the idea of lowering arrests may have come with good intentions, but a drop of 98% means very few are facing consequences. This sends the wrong message to all students.

City School Police Officer:
"These kids get up already with their backs against the wall. Most of them are trying to do the right thing of trying to get an education." "There is always one bad apple. If you don't correct that apple, it will continue to spiral in a negative way."

I'm Chris Papst, and this is Project Baltimore.

((END PACKAGE))

A drop of 98% in arrests and 62% in suspensions over a relatively short period of time? Perhaps *McDonalds* was correct. Data is king.

* * *

When we reported these massive drops in suspensions and arrests, school employees began contacting us in droves.

One City Schools nurse told us during an interview, "Going into these schools, it's heartbreaking, and that's the only way to describe it. It feels like you're going into a war."

"I'm thinking you have to be exaggerating," I replied, on camera.

"Absolutely not. The first thing we say is like, 'Here we are. We're in Afghanistan.' And that's how we feel. We feel like we're at war."

This nurse, like many school employees, wished not to be identified for fear of losing their job.

"We see the bigger picture." The nurse explained how the violence is daily and getting worse. Fractured jaws, concussions, head injuries, stitches—all of it from fights.

"The violence within Baltimore City Public Schools has reached an epidemic, and I don't think the alarms are being sounded," the nurse added. "I don't think people really realize just how violent and how much the violence has escalated within the previous years. It's just not publicized."

The nurse's frustration continued to mount. Nurses have a unique perspective on violence. To a nurse, these kids aren't numbers. They're patients.

"We've seen the violence, we've seen the escalation on a whole different level. And I know the numbers may say differently, that it's going downwards. But that's not what is going on in these schools. That's not what is going on in these buildings. It is actually just the opposite," said the nurse.

"Student behavior is out of control in our schools," explained one teacher we spoke with who had 25 years of teaching English in Baltimore City classrooms. In that time, this teacher had seen the devastating impact of bullying, violence and intimidation, which they said was escalating despite what the data show.

"Teachers have no authority at all anymore in the school," the teacher explained. "None. So we're just trying to hold back the tide, and we really aren't very successful at it a lot of the time. I get cussed out 10, 15, 20 times a day by students I don't even know. It's a very discouraging environment to work in when you hear the F-word, the B-word, the N-word, the S-word 1,000 times a day, and I'm not exaggerating."

"I see the children of Baltimore being failed," the teacher added. "They are not being provided an education, not being provided a safe environment, being left in a position where they will [not have] much of a future to look forward to unless something changes."

The school violence cover-up is by no means limited to Baltimore City Schools. We produced an extremely powerful story on an eight-year-old girl who was attacked at her Baltimore County school, Dogwood Elementary. The video we aired was hard to watch. The young girl had just returned home from school, and she was screaming. "I don't want to go to school! I don't want to go to school!" She yelled hysterically as her mother recorded on a phone.

"Why? Why? I'm tired of them." The young girl was hysterical. It was heartbreaking.

I asked the girl's mom why she would want to document such a terrible moment. "My first instinct, of course, as a mother was to grab her and hold her and to kiss her and to love her," she explained, tears running down her face. "But I felt like I needed to show this. I'm about to cry because I saw that video. But I knew that I had to do it for people to see me, to believe me."

The mom and daughter told me severe bullying had been a problem all year at Dogwood. The mom says her daughter regularly came home crying. But on this day, sitting on the family couch, this mom finally realized how much her child was suffering.

I asked the young girl why she was crying. She looked up at me with adorable, dark brown eyes. Like wide-open faucets, they dampened her shirt. "Because they treat me horribly."

As this little girl cried hysterically in the video, her mom noticed injuries to her head. The eight-year-old was rushed to the emergency room. A doctor at the Greater Baltimore Medical Center diagnosed her injuries as an "assault." One so bad that the ER doctor kept her out of school for the following three days. Baltimore County Police investigated and found the second grader was a victim of the crime, Assault in the Second Degree.

"I couldn't touch her head for days," said her mom, "I had to take her to her doctor that Friday. Her doctor couldn't even touch her head."

Citing this attack and repeated instances of violence, the girl's pediatrician sent a letter to the school's principal requesting a transfer, saying, "Dogwood Elementary is no longer capable of providing a safe environment."

But when the family filed a bullying complaint with the school, the result was very different. Despite the police report, the medical records and the doctor's note, which all describe a serious attack, the school determined, "There is not sufficient evidence to prove that your child was subjected to bullying or intimidation behaviors." No recommended discipline for the attacker. The mom flat-out called it a cover-up, saying the principal didn't want the incident documented. It made her school look unsafe.

"The boy was playing and he hit her in the head by mistake," the mom said incredulously and with disgust. "That's what the principal said."

The girl told police she was hit three times on the head.

The mom stated, "I feel the children are not safe in the schools anymore. If I had the money or the means to be able to do it, I would take her out of the school system altogether and put her somewhere private."

Project Baltimore contacted the school and district administration requesting an interview. We got an email saying, "We won't be making [Principal] Johari Toe available for interviews, nor will we be making anyone from Central Office available."

But we wanted answers for this little girl. So, we drove to the school shortly after dismissal and waited in a parking lot next to the school. Eventually, the principal came outside to update the message on the school's sign. While she was on the sidewalk in front of her school, my photographer and I approached her.

"Principal Toe. My name is Chris Papst from Fox45." She hadn't spotted us until I had already begun to introduce myself. The man next to her casually slid behind the sign, out of the camera's view.

"You don't have the right to record me," stated Toe. "You don't have the right to record me." She repeated as she tried to scurry away.

"We are on a public sidewalk," I quickly informed her.

In a panic, Toe made a beeline for the school's parking lot. I followed her and began asking my questions. My photographer followed closely behind. Our producer was staged in a nearby car getting wider angles of the "interview."

"Do you not think this is legitimate?" I was holding the police report in front of her so she could see it. "There is a police report about a second-degree assault that happened inside your school. You signed paperwork saying there's no evidence of intimidation or bullying."

The principal spun in a circle, quickly walked over some grass and then hopped a curb. She was clearly rattled and had no idea what to do. She tried to speed up and slow down. We just kept pace. With no direction or plan in mind, she pulled out her phone and appeared to call someone. I got the impression she was trying to appear busy on camera.

"A doctor had written a letter to you saying your school is not a safe environment for students," I continued. "Can we just ask you about your violence and bullying policy at your school?"

After a few U-turns and S-turns, Toe noticed an open door in the front of the school. She walked as fast as she could towards it, phone still pressed to her ear.

I just kept talking, "There's a police report about a second-degree assault."

When she got to the door, she slipped inside. "Please don't come into my school. You don't have the right to record any student at Dogwood Elementary. Please get off my school property. Thank you." The door then slammed shut, and Principal Toe was gone.

Shortly after the story aired, the mom who took the video pulled her daughter out of Dogwood.

"The problem is not just here, it's all over," the mom told me. "Something has to be done to stop this. It's horrible. Second grade, I should not have to be worrying about where to put my child next year."

Despite this mom's concerns and our attempts to get answers, Toe remained a principal in Baltimore County Schools, making $142,016 a year.

* * *

Back in Baltimore City Schools, when it began to decrease arrests and suspensions significantly, we noted how that action corresponded with an increase in bullying reports. This spike in bullying meant a spike in bullying victims. What struck me most while interviewing some of the victims was the lack of urgency coming from the school.

In most instances, it seems the teachers tried to stop the bullying. But when the situation reached the principal's or assistant principal's desk, the efforts ceased. I can't even tell you how many bullying victims have contacted Project Baltimore. The numbers are overwhelming. We interview as many as we can. In doing so, we've learned each student responds differently. One student told us the bullying got so bad, she made a decision that nearly cost her life.

Reality Adams was fourteen years old when we spoke with her. A robust girl who could pass for twenty. Dark eyes, dark hair, dark complexion with a bright smile.

"Reality is very outgoing. She is very funny." Nickey Adams beamed while looking at her daughter. Reality is the "heartbeat of the household," she told us.

"She is silly," laughed Nickey. "She's a great cook. I taught her and she outcooks me."

When we sat down with Reality, she didn't seem very silly or funny. She seemed depressed.

"She's been harassed, bullied, assaulted. It's just been a living hell, if I could say." Her mom's joy also vanished.

The eighth grader attended KIPP Ujima Village Academy and said bullying had been a problem for years. It got so bad, Reality admitted she's physically fought other students. Her mother has filed bullying complaints and sent emails to school leaders.

When we asked Reality questions about her school experience, she spoke softly, "This has been rough, going to school, staying focused, and then worrying about this. I can't go to the bathroom by myself. I don't go to the bathroom by myself."

The school's response to Reality's concerns was to hold mediation meetings with the students. It didn't seem to work.

"It makes me angry because she should feel safe in school." Nickey shook her head in disgust. "I just feel that that's unfair on her, and then you have the school saying, well, why don't you just transfer her. No! I feel like, why don't you fix the problem?" Nickey delivered her words with anger.

Towards the end of the school year, Reality explained to us that she got into an all-out fight with another girl in front of a school administrator.

"And he just pulls me away, telling me to calm down." Reality's voice rose in pitch, but was still soft. "It's not that serious? A girl just hit me, and you're right there. I came to you to avoid the situation. And you didn't do anything."

Reality was treated at Sinai Hospital for eye socket trauma. A school police report labeled the incident a common assault. Her mother filed a claim with the Department of Juvenile Services for alleged second-degree battery.

"It's just the school wasn't doing anything, and my mom tried everything." Reality's voice drew to a near whisper. "I seen her on the phone for hours: texting people, calling people, trying to get them to stop. And everything that we did or everything that we had done is not working, and they're still coming up to me . . ." She paused to collect her emotions. "And I'm like . . . I can't."

Then, Reality made a devastating decision. Ending her life to end the bullying.

Reality's mother did her best to compose herself while recalling the worst day of her life. "She's supposed to be sleeping in the next room. And her friend calls me, 2:00 in the morning to say, Ms. Nickey, Reality just took a lot of pills. And I'm asleep. So, I almost felt like I was dreaming. And I got up and I went into her room and she's just sitting on the end of the bed—like out of it. She's sitting up, but she's out of it. And I said, 'Did you take pills? Did you take pills?' And I seen the pills and I just immediately called the ambulance to come and get her."

"Did you think you were going to lose your daughter?" It was one of the hardest questions I had ever asked someone.

Nickey wiped a napkin on her eyes. "Yes. It was like moments of her whole life flashing all at one time: good, bad, parks, walks. It was just like a flash of all this stuff from her. And I was just like, I can't lose my baby like this. I can't lose my baby. I can't lose my baby."

I turned to Reality. She was sitting next to her mother. I didn't say anything. I just waited for her to speak.

"It was like my last night was going to be right now," whispered Reality. "Just seeing my mother's face, and I'm like that's the only person that I'm going to see, her and people at the hospital. I was going to put everything on the line—not being able to walk across the stage for my mom, not being able to have my own kids one day. I was just thinking about so much stuff. I'm not going to be able to get to high school with these girls. It's no point in me being here."

"You thought you were going to die." I didn't want to ask Reality that question while she was sitting next to her mother, but I felt I had to.

"I didn't feel myself," she responded, always looking at the ground. "I felt myself letting go."

Reality was rushed to the hospital. Her mother says her stomach was pumped. The eighth grader was placed on suicide watch for two days before returning home.

"She's fourteen." Nickey spoke much louder than her daughter. "A 14-year-old shouldn't even have those type of thoughts. She hasn't even lived her life. She has so much more life to live. That should be the furthest thing from her mind."

Weeks after the fight that led Reality to attempt suicide, a City Circuit Court judge issued peace orders against students at KIPP, ordering them to stay away from Reality. We didn't name the students in our story because they are minors. But Project Baltimore spoke to the families of two of the students, who told us it goes both ways. They claim, at times, that Reality was the aggressor. But they did not provide any documentation. Either way, one thing they all seem to agree on is that there is a problem at the school and it's not being handled.

KIPP, which is America's largest network of public charter schools, declined an interview but gave us this statement: "Since this situation was brought to our attention, KIPP Baltimore teachers and staff have addressed the concerns of the students involved and taken every step to ensure the safety of all students. In order to protect the privacy of our students, we are not at liberty to discuss the details of this case."

Reality's mother says the peace orders are a step in the right direction. But a piece of paper only does so much to keep her daughter safe.

"I want justice," explained Reality. "I want them to get the consequences they need to leave me alone. Like, they're not stopping. They don't care. Whatever we do, they don't care. They're still going to pick and pick and pick until something happens."

Baltimore City Schools also gave us a statement, saying that reports of bullying are taken extremely seriously. That appears to be the standard line from many schools.

When Reality's story aired, the community responded. It resonated strongly with other parents who contacted us, saying their children faced the same devastating decision.

"I have a 14-year-old daughter as well," said one caller. "She was cyberbullied, and some other things happened, and she as well wanted to take her life."

Another parent called and said this, "My son tried to commit suicide, and he's only seven."

Here's yet another parent speaking of the violence: "I don't know what to do. I'm thinking of not sending him to school, and I can get put in jail for that."

The desperation in the parents' voices was more alarming than their words.

"I feel like if the school sees a pattern of a certain student that's a constant issue, they should be removed. But they don't," stated Reality's mom during our interview. "I liked the school because the school has had a good reputation. And now I'm starting to feel like, well, their reputation was only good because they were keeping everything hidden."

* * *

Reality's story was a difficult one to hear. Afterward, the drive back to the office was quiet. Following that type of interview, a lot goes through a journalist's head. It's our job to report, and we have deadlines. So, immediately, following an interview, we're thinking about story construction, outlines, leads, soundbites, and promotion. But we're also human. As much as we try to stay objective, emotional reactions happen. I hated hearing what happened to Reality and her family. What bothered me most was that it seemed largely preventable.

Naturally, you start pondering who's at fault. Is it the eighth-grade girls? Is it their parents? Is it the school? The answer, likely, to an extent, is all three. But the bullying happened at KIPP when parents were not around. And kids will do whatever adults allow.

But a child's reaction to adult inaction isn't always negative. We found a Baltimore girl who, at age nine, used her bullying experience as motivation to do something most people don't do in a lifetime.

Rianna Facey was your everyday third grader at Calvin Rodwell Elementary in Northwest Baltimore. She liked her friends, gymnastics and track. She also loved the book *The Cat That Wouldn't Go Away*.

We learned about Rianna from a viewer tip. We then called her mom, asking her to tell her daughter's story. Soon after, we met the nine-year-old at her home and recorded her reading the book. "Have you ever met a cat that wouldn't go away? I did." The joy she got out of reading the book was heartwarming. "It was the middle of May when a cat showed up on my porch one day. Guess what? He wouldn't go away. When I looked out my window, he was there. When I opened the door, he was there. 'MEOW.'"

As she read the book, her mother, Tywanna Gardner, sat next to her on the front steps of their home, beaming!

"I asked my mom what he wanted, and he was here. She thought he was lost and belonged to another neighbor. I thought the cat was looking for toys, so I ran up to my room and brought him down toys. He sniffed them and walked away. 'What's wrong with this cat? Who doesn't like toys?' I asked. A neighbor nearby said, 'He's hungry, he's looking for food.'"

Rianna paused and looked up at her mother, seeking approval. "Is that good?"

Her mom smiled widely with a slight nod.

"My mom went to the store and brought the cat some food. A man working in the area said 'Now he'll never go away.' The cat ate the food like he hadn't eaten in months."

She turned the page.

"Day after day, he walked me to the car. He walked me to the house. I thought he would walk me to a little mouse."

Rianna stopped, took a slow breath and slowed her reading. Her countenance turned serious.

"Everywhere I went, the cat followed. One day, my mom saw the cat being bullied by other cats. They surrounded him. One cat went towards him and knocked him into the street. The little cat ran away, he didn't give up though, he came back another day."

Her joy returned.

"It's August now, and the cat is still here. He won't go away. I guess he'll stay. If you meet a cat that won't go away, I hope your cat is friendly."

She then read the book's title, *The Cat That Wouldn't Go Away*, by Rianna Facey.

Rianna fell in love with writing at a summer learning camp at a Baltimore City school. She began jotting down stories in a journal.

When a cat showed up one day on her front porch, her inspiration was born. A family friend provided illustrations. Then the nine-year-old went online, found a self-publisher, and this Baltimore City student became a published author.

"I'm really proud of her." Tywanna didn't have to say she was proud; it was obvious. "She's only nine and wrote the book when she was eight. It's something I didn't do."

We didn't learn this until a few months later. But Rianna's story was based on her own real-life bullying experience. She hid her pain in the pages of a book.

"One day, my mom saw the cat being bullied by other cats," The book stated. "They surrounded him. One cat went towards him and knocked him into the street."

Tywanna explained, "She put in the book that the cat was bullied, but the reason she did it is because she was bullied."

"It kind of made me feel like I was unwanted," said Rianna. A nine-year-old girl said she felt unwanted at school. How awful.

Rianna said she had endured bullying for years. Her mom said it got so bad, Rianna came to her one day with a heartbreaking confession.

Tywanna looked down at her daughter with pity, "You said you thought about suicide when you came out of school that Friday."

Like Reality, Rianna had considered ending her life to end the bullying.

"It's just horrible. It's devastating. Children shouldn't have to go through that," cried Tywanna.

In that moment, Tywanna realized how much her daughter needed help. She encouraged her to write down her thoughts and feelings, and she did. Her own experience with bullying became the inspiration for her book.

"I didn't think it would be a book, you know, I just thought she would write it on paper and throw it away, but it helped her," declared Tywanna. "I think it saved her life. Writing about the cat."

Rianna's mother told us that writing that story and sharing it with Project Baltimore is the reason the school finally intervened.

"I think they just kind of hoped it would go away," said Tywanna, speaking of the school's response to bullying. "And they didn't take it seriously, like they should have. Because it went on too long. Years is too long for bullying to go on for anyone."

"Maybe she can help somebody by letting people know her story," added Tywanna. "I'm thankful that she's alive, that she's not another kid on the news that committed suicide."

During the two interviews we did with Rianna. We had a hard time getting her to talk. She was very quiet. But not shy. This was a girl who better expressed herself through the written word.

But one of the few things she did say was, "I just want my mom to be okay."

Tywanna wrapped her arms around her daughter and squeezed. "I'm okay. I'm just glad you're okay."

But remember, arrests in Baltimore City Schools are down 98%. And far fewer students are being suspended. Schools must be safer. That is, if you believe the data.

CHAPTER 6

WHAT ONCE WAS

Baltimore City Schools hasn't always been this way.

In July 1908, a boy named Thoroughgood was born in Baltimore. At the time, Baltimore was America's seventh-largest city with around 550,000 residents and growing fast. Thoroughgood was the descendant of slaves on both sides of his family. His father worked on the railroads.

His mother was a teacher. The young man, according to numerous reports, learned how to debate from his father. Within him was instilled a love of the law and the court process.

At the time, Baltimore, like much of America, was segregated. The city had two high schools where African Americans could enroll, Frederick Douglass and Paul Laurence Dunbar. Thoroughgood attended Douglass, where he graduated in 1925. He then went to Lincoln University in Pennsylvania. In 1929, he got married. A year later, he graduated.

Fate took him to Howard University School of Law, where he said his mother pawned her wedding ring to pay for his tuition. In 1933, he graduated first in his class. Thoroughgood then went into private practice in Baltimore before founding the NAACP Legal Defense and Education Fund. Eventually, Thoroughgood Marshall changed his name to Thurgood Marshall. It was under that name that he argued several cases before the U.S. Supreme Court, including Brown v. Board of Education.

In 1961, President John Kennedy appointed Marshall to the United States Court of Appeals for the Second Circuit. A few years later, President Lyndon Johnson appointed Marshall as the United States Solicitor General and then successfully nominated him as the first African American justice of the United States Supreme Court. Marshall served in that position until 1991 and died two years later.

Marshall's remarkable life began in Baltimore City Public Schools. The first African American justice on the Supreme Court graduated from a segregated Frederick Douglass High School. And by all accounts, he received a quality education. Ninety years later, in 2017, an unsegregated Frederick Douglass High School was one of those six city schools that failed to produce one student who scored proficient in any state testing. What happened?

I wasn't alive 90 years ago; I can't compare the educational standards and expectations of then to now. But I do know this, in Maryland, funding equals educational success in the eyes of many, including most of this state's politicians.

In 2021, the Maryland legislature overrode then-Governor Larry Hogan's veto and passed the largest public education spending increase in the state's history. It was called The Blueprint for Maryland's Future, based on the recommendation of the Kirwan Commission. The bill increases school funding by $32 billion over the first 10 years and then $4 billion every year after that. The legislation did not come with a funding mechanism. But the bill is law. So, it must be funded.

I could take the next few pages and quote all the politicians who promised the extra funding would produce more educated students. Maybe it will. I sure hope it does. If this doesn't work and the economic benefits are not realized, how is the state going to pay for it? Future taxpayers will have to generate the additional revenue. If the state produces more doctors, lawyers, tradesmen and tech professionals—jobs that increase the tax base—the Blueprint will pay for itself. If that doesn't happen, the state will have tough fiscal choices to make.

But when looking at Kirwan's funding increases and the political promises, we do have a comparison. Twenty years before the Kirwan Commission, Maryland had the Thornton Commission. At the time, it was the largest education spending increase in Maryland history.

The year was 2002. The political title of the bill was The Bridge to Excellence in Public Schools Act. Sounds great, right? Who could be against that? But most people just called it Thornton. And it was heavily debated.

"With regards to Thornton, I can pay for it, you can't. We're $1.7 billion in the hole. If you're going to advocate a massive tax increase, let's do it now," said former Governor Bob Ehrlich during a gubernatorial debate in 2002.

Back then, Maryland was spending $8,921 per student, per year, according to the U.S. Census—about $900 more than the national average ($8,019). But Thornton dramatically increased that amount. By 2020 (the year before Kirwan passed), Maryland was spending $15,489 per pupil—about $2,000 more than the U.S. average ($13,494). As taxes went up, taxpayers were promised, more funding means better schools.

Baltimore City's spending per pupil also greatly increased. Thornton passed in 2002. By 2011, of the 100 largest school districts in America, Baltimore City was the third most funded in terms of per-pupil spending, according to the U.S. Census. And it's largely stayed there since, with some variation. LA, Miami and Houston are here for comparison. They are not near the top.

2011 Per Pupil Spending

New York City $19,710
Boston $19,181
Baltimore City $15,483
Los Angeles $10,904
Miami $9,059
Houston $8,984

"If you focus on education. If you put good money into it and you have excellent management and fabulous teachers, you can make a difference," stated Kathleen Kennedy Townsend, who was running against Ehrlich in 2002. She lost.

Decades later, did that extra money make a difference? In 2003, Maryland's high school graduation rate was 84 percent, ten points above the national average, according to the National Center for Education Statistics. By 2019, Maryland jumped to 87 percent. But, on average, the rest of America did better, too. By 2022, Maryland's graduation rate fell to 86 percent, one point below the national average of 87 percent.

	2003	2019	2022
Maryland	84%	87%	86%
U.S. Average	74%	86%	87%

What about test scores? As we discussed earlier, every two years, the federal government releases what's known as The Nation's Report Card, or the National Assessment of Educational Progress (NAEP). All students get similar tests, so it's a fair comparison across the nation. In 2003, the combined average of Maryland's math and English scores was one point above the national average. Nearly 20 years later, after taxes went up and billions of additional dollars went to Maryland schools, test scores in 2022 fell to three points below the national average. In 2024, Maryland was one point below the national average. To be fair, overall education spending across the country skyrocketed. But Maryland's skyrocketed more. And both got worse.

NAEP Scores	2003	2022	2024
National Average	247	245	245
Maryland	248	242	244

Baltimore City joined NAEP in 2009. As we mentioned, by 2011, City Schools was the third most funded large school system in America. Here are the scores. From 2009 to 2024, Baltimore City's scores went down 11 points. The large city average went down two points. In 2019, the year before COVID, Baltimore City was down five points. The large city average was up three points in that same time period. In other words, Baltimore City hit an all-time low when compared to the big city average.

NAEP Scores	2009	2019	2022	2024
Baltimore City	231	226	218	220
Large City Average	241	244	239	239

"I would ask, where are the results?" Jennifer Butler, with the Maryland Public Policy Institute, a center-right think tank, says the results are clear: money is simply not the answer.

"There is absolutely no correlation between the amount of money invested in schools and the results and test grades. I mean, we've seen scandal after scandal in Baltimore City, and I would ask, is the money that they currently have being used effectively and efficiently? I think the answer is no. So before we start talking about putting more money into a failing school district, maybe we need to stop and take a look at what they're already doing with what they have," said Butler.

"These are the right questions to be asking, absolutely." Delegate Eric Luedtke, a Democrat from Montgomery County, was a member of the Kirwan Commission. Luedtke says that, since 2002, Maryland's number of students living in poverty has drastically increased, along with our special education needs and the number of English language learners.

"So, the fact that our graduation rates and our NAEP rates have not done worse is a testament to what happened in Thornton," stated Luedtke.

But when Thornton was being debated, there were no caveats attached to the money. And I'm sure plenty of other states also saw increases in English language learners and poverty rates.

Kirwan supporters say the bill is more than just a massive influx of new educational dollars. It increases teacher salaries to attract better teachers, encourages teachers to obtain a high level of certification, expands pre-k and increases oversight and accountability of how the additional money is spent. In 2002, when Thornton was being debated, politicians made similar arguments, saying it's more than just money. Taxpayers were also promised it would work. Judging by the NAEP scores, it didn't.

"We can do better with more investment," explained Luedtke. "We're not just increasing funding. We're reforming schools. And we're providing a new structure of accountability to make sure the schools are doing the best they can for our kids."

Think back to a segregated Frederick Douglass High School in 1925. How much funding do you think it received, compared to what it receives today? Yet, it produced a historical figure like Thurgood Marshall. How does that happen? When I asked that question to one city mom, she gave me her honest opinion. And it had nothing to do with money.

* * *

As a local journalist, I feel it's important to educate myself about the community I cover. So, I occasionally schedule meetings with local advocacy groups in the city. Most of these groups are African American. One group is called MOMS, Mothers of Murdered Sons. As the name implies, it's a survivor's support network.

On a warm spring afternoon, my producer and I drove to West Baltimore and met with about a dozen members. They asked a lot about Project Baltimore and its goals. We asked about their struggles, successes and desires. It was a candid conversation about reality. My producer and I were the only white people in the room. And we asked sincere and sometimes uncomfortable questions. My goal was to learn. In order to report on the issues in Baltimore effectively, I need to understand those issues. That meant I needed to know the "how."

How did Baltimore become one of the deadliest cities in America? How did it become one of America's poorest cities? How did Frederick Douglass High School go from graduating Thurgood Marshall to having zero students proficient in state testing? How did the city get to this point?

The members of MOMS discussed those questions for about twenty minutes with varying opinions. They spoke about redlining, the highway system, white flight, systemic racism, and so on. The conversation was passionate. I learned a lot. Then, the conversation instantly changed when one woman spoke above all the other voices.

"I'll tell you how it happened." All eyes shifted to her. She was an older African American lady in bright clothes. Like everyone else in the group, her child was murdered.

"I'll tell you exactly how it happened." She leaned back in her chair with confidence, as if her coming words could not be challenged. "The worst thing to ever happen to the black community was desegregation."

Half the room erupted in clapping, while the other half gasped.

"That's right!" She hollered. "Desegregation did all this. Think about it," she said, sitting up tall. "Before desegregation, our schools were better. Our families were stronger. We had jobs. We were a community."

"How could you possibly say that?" hollered one lady in disgust.

The woman whipped her head towards the question. "Look around. This community didn't look like this sixty years ago." She slouched back in her chair, turning to me. Her voice softened to mirror her countenance. "When we were segregated, we were together. We looked out for each other. We protected each other. When desegregation happened, people started leaving. Most everyone who was successful left. All the positive role models and mentors for our young people, left. They moved outside the city—because they could." She paused as her challengers remained silent. "After everyone left, we had nothing left."

She gestured with her hands, as if to encircle the blighted neighborhood that surrounded us.

"*That* is how this happened."

* * *

My conversation with MOMS has always stuck with me, especially considering who I met shortly after. Her name was Christine Bryant. Bryant, an older African American lady, had recently retired as a teacher and was getting ready to leave the city. Her small apartment was partially packed when we arrived. Bryant had a teacher's mentality, no nonsense with a sense of humor, all wrapped up in matronly attire.

"I know I'm getting myself in trouble," she said as she sat down for the interview. "Somebody has to speak up."

When I asked her about the "how," she did not hold back. How did Baltimore City schools become one of the lowest-performing school systems in America, even though it's among the most funded?

"I think it's a gross mismanagement of money," Bryant stated bluntly, but not proudly. "We had roof leaks. Mice in the fluorescent lights. Yes. Yes."

For 17 years, Bryant had devoted her working life to teaching some of Baltimore City's most disadvantaged kids. When she retired, she couldn't stay quiet.

"I want to be heard," she said. "I wanted people to know that there is someone out here for your children."

Bryant was a STEM teacher. But she told me she routinely had no supplies. She had to buy even the basics like paper, pencils and whiteboard markers. Teachers can deduct, on their Federal Income Taxes, $300 a year for classroom expenses. But Bryant says she would spend that much in one month. On top of that, with up to 32 students per class, her room didn't have enough desks. Students sat on top of tables. The windows were broken. The bathrooms never had paper towels. Janitors were so hard to get. She kept a mop and broom to clean her own room, which included picking up mouse feces.

As a science teacher, her faucets didn't have hot water. When the Internet went down, it took North Avenue days for someone to fix it. During winter, the thermostat would break, and her classroom would have no heat.

"There is something being done wrong," said Bryant. "I feel like the children are being left behind because the focus is more on the adults. I saw a lot and I tried to change a lot. But one voice is not going to be heard."

"We are losing a whole generation of kids in this city. A whole generation," stated Bryant, who was clearly troubled by what she had witnessed during her career. "My major concern was to see the children grow. I loved to see their faces light up when they got it."

To Bryant, that was the best part of the job—seeing the sudden joy when a student finally understands what had previously not been understood. But she said between those moments, there was a lot of frustration brought about by bad leadership.

"What I see is that we are fixing one thing and putting band aids on things. Whereas, we are not looking at the whole foundation of the problem."

"I always told the administrators it was the students. I was there for the students," Bryant said.

"Do you feel the administrators were there for the students?" I asked.

Bryant's tired eyes dropped as she released a long sigh.

"That's a rough question." Bryant raised her head. "No. I have to be honest."

* * *

Bryant's message was powerful. And she agreed to deliver it on TV. She didn't fear retaliation. She had already retired. Afterwards, Bryant's principal fired back.

The principal demanded that we interview her. So, we did. We set up our interview at a time when no students were in school. We placed two chairs in the middle of a long hallway lined with lockers. The school itself looked good. I didn't see any mice. It looked clean. It smelled fine. But all the classroom doors were shut. We were only allowed to roam a small section of the hallways.

"I'm here, ready to speak on behalf of our community, our staff, our students, to say we have a great school," began principal Omotayo Abiodun, who said she was shocked by Bryant's claims.

Abiodun patrolled the halls of Garrett Heights Elementary as its proud principal for eight years.

Garrett Heights was a school that struggled. Attendance is low. Test scores are below the district average, which is already low. Basic supplies, like paper and pencils, are so hard to come by; local churches and the PTA donate them. The school claimed to have so little money, it cut its basketball team. Despite the adversity, Abiodun felt compelled to defend herself.

"It just does not represent who we are," she said. "We have teachers, and we have staff, and we have different types of personnel that do become frustrated, that's absolutely the truth, but you also have people who get over those frustrations and do what's best for kids every day."

I asked Abiodun about Bryant's claim that school administrators did not prioritize students.

"I could see where maybe that would be the perception, but that's not the reality," replied Abiodun. "We work through our breaks, we work through our weekends, just trying to support the vision of our schools. I just want to say that we have worked extremely hard, and that's not often shared; the negative information is shared. But you have got people who are committed to the city, committed to the children and the communities to make this work happen, and so I think that's what I'm here to share."

Abiodun said she wanted to turn Garrett Heights into a charter school, which would give her more freedom and flexibility with educating her students. But she wouldn't get that chance.

Two months after Abiodun defended her school on the news, she was removed as principal. I asked North Avenue why. I was told, "It is the practice of the district not to comment on personnel matters. The status of a principal's employment with the district is considered a personnel matter."

I have no evidence to suggest Abiodun was replaced because of the interview. I also have no evidence to suggest she wasn't. But I do know this, since 2017, very few city schools' principals have interviewed with Project Baltimore. Most lost their jobs soon after.

* * *

As you read the previous chapters, did anything stick out to you as strangely coincidental?

In 2002, Maryland politicians dumped billions of additional tax dollars into public education (The Thornton Plan). Taxpayers were promised a return on that investment. This was a political gamble. For politicians to keep their jobs, it was vital that school data improve. So, is it possible this educational bet was hedged?

Between 2003 and 2022, federal standardized test scores in Maryland (NAEP) went down in math and reading, which we discussed earlier. Yet, at the same time, high school graduation rates statewide increased from 84% in 2003 to 86% in 2022.

How can that happen?

As *McDonalds* pointed out, public officials cannot easily manipulate standardized test scores. But they can influence statewide graduation rates. Remember, in 2007, Maryland instituted "Bridge Projects." Around that same time, lower-performing school systems adopted policies like "The 50% Rule" and the "one fail rule."

The result? Graduation rates went up, even though student proficiencies in math and reading went down.

Winners and losers.

NOTE: Remember, in 2021, Maryland again significantly increased education funding with the Blueprint for Maryland's Future. What did state leaders do to hedge that educational bet? Stay tuned.

C H A P T E R   7

"WILLFULLY AND KNOWINGLY"

Over the previous few chapters, we discussed many educational issues facing Baltimore City Schools students, staff and families. That context is valuable in understanding why our 2017 public records lawsuit against the district was so important. I understand some of what we highlighted in the last few chapters was more recent. But it's those types of historical and systemic issues that convinced us that the lawsuit was necessary. City Schools was willing to spend massive amounts of taxpayer dollars to hide the truth from taxpayers. But in this case, taxpayers won.

Baltimore City Schools "willfully and knowingly" violated the law. That's a powerful statement. But it's not mine. Those words belong to Baltimore City Judge Jeannie Hong.

Fifteen months after Project Baltimore sued Baltimore City Schools for violating Maryland's public records law, the case went to trial. I never anticipated taking this case all the way to court. But the school system left us no choice. On February 11, 2019, Judge Hong heard ten hours of testimony. I testified on the stand for about two hours. The following month, March 2019, Judge Hong issued her ruling. And it was damning. The judge said the school system *knew* they were breaking the law by not releasing the documents, and they did it anyway.

Our argument before the court was simple. From the beginning, we believed parents and taxpayers had a right to see the documents we requested. Remember, this all started with a simple public records request after we reported on allegations of grade changing at a Baltimore City school. North Avenue, in 2017, refused to release anything. Fifteen months later, in 2019, a judge forced them.

"It's a victory for teachers, parents, taxpayers, but most of all, students. I hope that this is the first step towards some accountability over there on North Avenue," said Scott Marder, the attorney who represented us in the case.

"When I looked at this from the beginning and saw that they had no basis to deny your requests, how frivolous the denials were, and then when I saw what happened over the weeks after we filed suit, it was almost a foregone conclusion that this is what was gonna happen, and it's a shame. It didn't have to come to this," stated Marder.

"The judge heard all of the evidence," continued Marder, "and found not just that the school system mistakenly violated the law, but that they *intentionally* violated the law. That was a very important, very significant finding."

In Judge Hong's ruling, she said the quality of education in Baltimore City Public Schools is of the utmost importance to the public. She then delivered that powerful statement, saying City Schools "willfully and knowingly" violated the law by not handing over the documents, and that decision may have been to "hide possible wrongdoing." Judge Hong ruled that the "defendant failed to turn over or submit documents it knew to be responsive to the MPIA request."

This was not just a win for Project Baltimore. This was a smackdown of the school system.

Fox45 reached out to City Schools after the ruling. The district declined an interview, but gave us this statement that read:

"We believe the Court's ruling will have a chilling effect on investigations. Staff members, students, parents, and other members of the community should be able to have reasonable assurance of confidentiality. Without it, they will be less likely to report concerns."

City Schools made that same argument many times in court. The judge outright rejected it.

"Decisions like this are critical to accountability in government. Oftentimes, the government will think that it's above the law, and in this case, the judge said in fact that the school system thought they were above the law," explained Marder. "When I saw the ruling, I was elated because I believe in accountability, and government cannot run amok."

Judge Hong ruled City Schools must hand over *everything* we asked for in our initial 2017 public records request. The court ruled in our favor on every single order . . . all eight. Not only did the judge order North Avenue to hand over all the documents, but she also ordered the records to be unredacted, except for personal information. She also ordered the district to conduct a broader global search for what we requested. Finally, Judge Hong fined Baltimore City Schools $1,000. She then forced the district to reimburse Fox45's legal fees—nearly $200,000.

"The purpose of a public records law is to hold government accountable. This is an example of that happening, and there needs to be more of it, particularly here with the school system," added Marder. "It's a tragedy what's happened with our kids. When you look at the numbers, it's extraordinary. Had the school board litigated this case without filing frivolous papers in court, the legal fees would not have been nearly as high."

Baltimore City Schools is constantly asking taxpayers for more money. We've discussed how its classrooms don't have basic supplies like paper and pencils. Schools don't have heat when it's cold, or air conditioning when it's hot. Yet, North Avenue chose to spend hundreds of thousands of dollars to fight us in court. A case they were certain to lose and did.

"This opinion should have a huge impact on what the school system does. The judge very directly told them what they did was wrong. It's gonna cost them a lot of money, and I don't think they're gonna want to be in this position again," said Marder.

A few days after the ruling, I sat down with then-Governor Larry Hogan and Lt. Governor Boyd Rutherford. This was the first interview they had done together since taking office five years earlier. We met in the

Governor's reception room, a centuries-old, ornately decorated symbol of governmental self-significance.

"Knowingly and willfully violated the law. I thought, first of all, it didn't come as a shock to me," said Hogan.

"I wasn't surprised at all," said Rutherford.

I didn't expect Maryland's two top elected officials to come out so strongly. But they did. I barely asked any questions. The two just went off.

"The arrogance of some of these school systems to say we don't care, we don't have to answer your questions, and we don't have to provide you information, it's outrageous," said Hogan.

"Accountability is key," Rutherford followed. "They're not accountable to any elected official, and they should be."

Hogan picked it up. "When you hear teachers say we've gotta reach into our pockets to pay for school supplies, or when you hear parents saying our kids are freezing or sweating in a classroom, those are real problems. But it's not because they're not getting billions of dollars in funding. It's because of incompetence and mismanagement and a complete lack of accountability and the wasting of money."

"I think there's a systemic problem on North Avenue," said Rutherford, "in terms of the amount of money that goes into Baltimore City Schools, at least to North Avenue, it's not reaching the classroom. So, there are more people there that really need to be held accountable."

"Sadly," Hogan stated, "it was just a terrible decision on their part not to provide you the information that you deserved and that the public deserved to have. And it's a lot of money. But it's a drop in the bucket compared to the other millions of dollars, tens of millions of dollars that are being wasted on North Avenue and the Baltimore City School System. If we're gonna provide more investment in our local schools, they need to be more accountable to the state taxpayers."

* * *

The court's decision did more than just hand Fox45 a win. It also raised serious questions about the strength of Maryland's Public Information Act. When the district refused to give Project Baltimore documents, we had the means to challenge them in a courtroom. Most parents don't have that option. If a massive school system chooses to violate the law and withhold information from parents about their child's education, what can those parents do? It turns out, not much.

Baltimore City Schools is a billion-dollar organization with high-powered attorneys. Most parents, especially those in the city, don't have the resources to hire an attorney.

"The whole point of the lawsuit was that you made public records requests. Under Maryland law, you are entitled to those documents. They should have given them to you without you having to hire a law firm and sue them," said Marder. "What are regular people supposed to do? The purpose of the public records law is so government doesn't operate in secret. People have a right to know what their government is doing."

I also asked that question to Damon Effingham of Common Cause, a self-described, non-partisan think tank that works to strengthen Maryland's public information act.

"Well, the unfortunate thing is that there are really only two avenues," explained Effingham.

The first option, he said, is to contact the state's public records ombudsman, whose job is to assist in the process. But that position has no authority to order the release of information. If that avenue fails, Effingham says the only other thing parents can do in Maryland is file a lawsuit.

"That's very expensive and time-consuming, and for a typical Maryland parent, they don't have the time or the knowledge or the finances to be able to do that and to get this disclosure," said Effingham.

In 2014, Common Cause worked to improve Maryland's public records law. Some changes were made, but Effingham says it's not enough. He argues the law needs more teeth. The ombudsman needs more power, and there needs to be more uniformity.

"What we want is to not give these agencies any wiggle room to say we're interpreting it (the law) in our own way, which is what is really happening across the board right now," Effingham said.

Here's an example of what Effingham means. Project Baltimore files a lot of public records requests. I probably file a few a month. Maybe more. One request I regularly file involves "travel expenses." It's common for media entities to file this request to learn if anyone in government is living a little too lavishly on the taxpayer dollar. But when we file the request, each school system will give us something different.

Howard County Public Schools is the neighboring school system to the west of Baltimore. One time, I filed a request for "travel expenses," and Howard County Schools gave me everything. I could see each dollar the district spent on travel during the previous year. But when I sent that same request to Baltimore County Public Schools, we didn't get the documents. Instead, we got a bill stating it would cost $34,000 to release the records. Same request. Same state law. Different results.

Everywhere I've worked, bureaucratic machines twist and distort public records laws in search of ways to deny requests. And most states don't have sufficient teeth in the statutes to hold public agencies accountable to the law when it's violated.

"Transparency is the most foundational piece of holding government accountable. If you're not able to see the machinations of government that's supposed to be working for you, they can get away with anything," added Effingham.

"They could have probably, in the end, saved themselves a lot of trouble by just following the law," added Lucy Dalglish. At the time, Dalglish was still the Dean of the Philip Merrill College of Journalism at the University of Maryland. As an expert in public records law, we interviewed Dalglish a few times during the lawsuit.

"[The judge] knew that [the City Schools] did things they weren't supposed to. She allowed statutory damages, she allowed attorney's fees, which in Maryland does not happen as often as it does in most states that allow the recovery of attorney's fees. And she referred it for disciplinary action," explained Dalglish. "I rarely see that."

Judge Hong, in her ruling, stated North Avenue acted "arbitrarily and capriciously" in withholding the public records, and she ordered City Schools to "take disciplinary action." Has anyone been disciplined? City Schools sent us this statement, which states, "Baltimore City takes the judge's order very seriously. We reviewed staff activity and have complied with the judge's orders." In other words, they won't tell us.

However, with this ruling, we were set to learn a lot about what was actually happening inside City Schools. Remember those 106 fully-redacted pages? They were all from grade-changing investigations. With

Judge Hong's ruling, we would now be able to read them. We would also get the results of other grade-changing investigations, and emails, that North Avenue did not want the public to see.

"Anybody who's having difficulty getting a public record in Maryland will find this opinion very useful," added Dalglish. "It sets a roadmap for the test that you have to meet before you can block the release of a record."

The judge issued her ruling nineteen months after Project Baltimore first filed its public records request. For nineteen months, we kept asking ourselves the question: Why would City Schools fight us for so long and spend so much money to hide records?

Now, we would find out.

CHAPTER 8

NO ANSWERS?

For most parents, learning their child has been promoted to the next grade is good news. But not for Ciara Ford.

"I think that it's terrible," she cried. "I couldn't believe that he had passed. I was shocked, and I was kind of upset."

We interviewed Ford in her West Baltimore row home. She was a single mom trying desperately to raise her son and daughters in a tough area of town. Her neighborhood bore the deep-rooted scars that often form following years of violence, neglect and decay. Her row home was one of the few on her block that was still livable—and occupied. The rest had been boarded up or burned down.

Ford's son spent his third-grade year at Mary Ann Winterling Elementary in West Baltimore. The year had not gone well. He failed all of his classes, except one. He was absent or late to school 147 days, almost every day. His mom said the school assured her that he would stay in the third grade, which she wanted.

"It's not hurting them, it's helping them in the long run," she stated.

The problem for Ford is that it didn't happen. When she received her son's end-of-year report card, she learned he was promoted to fourth grade.

"What's the point of having passing and failing if you can fail every class and still pass? It's mindboggling," said Ford.

I asked her what message this sent to her son.

She replied in disgust, "That he doesn't have to work hard. He can do whatever he wants and still be promoted."

As I interviewed Ford, I wondered if her son was the byproduct of the "one fail rule," where "students cannot be retained a second time prior to ninth grade." Had Ford's son been held back in the third grade, so he couldn't be held back again? This was a student who failed almost every single class and was late or absent 147 days. Yet, the school passed him? How else can that be explained?

And Ford did not make any excuses. She did not defend her son's poor attendance. In fact, she said her son needed to be sent a strong message.

"I feel like they are setting him up for failure. How can he pass on to the next grade if he didn't grasp the concept of the grade that he was in? I think that is doing a disservice to my son," she added. "He's a very smart and bright kid, but he didn't do what he was supposed to do this year. But instead of holding him back and letting him get the concept of the third grade before promoting him, they promoted him. That is not the message I want to send."

What happened to Ford's son has real-life, future consequences. Remember Michelle Bradley? Parents like Ford and Gregory Gray, whom we discussed in Chapter One, understand that. Their priority is their children's education. But both parents felt the school system did not share that same priority. And when we began receiving the records following our court victory, that "feeling" for many was no longer . . . a feeling.

* * *

After an 18-month-long court battle, City Schools was now being forced by a judge to do what it fought hard to prevent—give us what we wanted. And the records did not disappoint.

Within the first batch of documents we received, there were plenty of headlines. Here's the first. In court, during the trial, the school's attorneys testified publicly that City Schools had eleven internal grade-changing investigations within the time frame of our request, which was about five years. The school's attorneys told the judge, *under oath*, that there were eleven grade-changing investigations. Turns out, that wasn't true.

When the district released the records, we received 22 grade-changing investigations. This was stunning. Had we not sued and won, the public would likely never have known the truth. And what was in those additional eleven internal reports was damning. Each one involved grade changing. But many involved other allegations.

In the reports, here is some of what we found.

- A principal spent $30,000 in school funds on Washington Wizards basketball tickets.
- The same principal bought gifts, including Smart TVs, Bose speakers, iPads, and a clothes dryer.
- City Schools' own investigator called the rounding up of failing grades to passing an "unwritten practice." The investigator went on to write in the report, "It is recommended that any previous 'practices' by BCPS personnel of rounding up failing grades to a passing grade be eliminated."
- Of the 22 grade-changing investigations, six confirmed serious allegations (and remember, this is City Schools investigating City Schools).
- Allegations of grade changing at Calverton Elementary/ Middle (the school where the principal sent that text) were substantiated.
  ◦ In the report, 386 grade change entries were made at Calverton during the 16/17 school year.
  ◦ Ten of the thirteen teachers interviewed said their grades were changed without their knowledge or consent.
  ◦ The investigator substantiated the allegation of "misconduct and neglect of duty for improper grade changes."
  ◦ Despite the results of the internal investigation, Calverton Principal Martia Cooper (as of 2024) is still employed by City Schools as an assistant principal, making about $142,515 a year.

- Concerning the NACA investigation (where we had that test), City Schools found the allegations to be unsubstantiated. Why? Because, according to the report, the investigation wasn't about *whether* grades were being changed. The allegations centered on whether the principal "directed and/or had knowledge of any grade changing." Those are very different things. And despite the investigator's efforts, that principal "elected not to be interviewed by anyone from Baltimore City Public Schools." Out of NACA II's 17 teachers, just four were questioned in what the investigator called an "extensive investigation." Also, in the NACA report, the investigator writes that rounding up failing grades to passing is an "unwritten practice" which occurs not just at NACA II, but "within the Baltimore City Public School system."

Now that we knew grade changing was widespread, it was time to ask school leadership some questions. And if they wouldn't agree to come to us, we would go to them.

* * *

200 E. North Avenue, Baltimore, MD 21202

The Alice G. Pinderhughes Administration Building, better known as the Baltimore City Public Schools' central office, or locally as just "North Avenue." This magnificent building, encompassing an entire city block, houses the district's hierarchy, including the Board of Commissioners. It's the medieval archetype of a shining castle encircled by a depressed village. With a four-story arched stone foyer, it out-classes many city town halls. Clearly, the building's construction coincided with the wealth Baltimore once possessed.

Inside North Avenue, public school board meetings are held twice a month. All of them are broadcast online. So, I don't often attend in person. But sometimes I'm forced to.

You see, after we received the first batch of records from the lawsuit, we made repeated interview requests with district leadership. We felt taxpayers deserved answers. When all of our requests were denied, we went to the only place where we knew district leaders would be. And we had a plan to ensure our questions were asked.

To make sure we didn't miss our opportunity, we arrived at North Avenue early. A few minutes later, right on cue, the elevator door dinged open. A member of City Schools' communication team hustled towards us. It was not Edie. She had long retired.

"Chris, can I help you?" she asked, a bit flustered. We did not inform them we were coming.

"No," I replied. "We're just here for the school board meeting."

She now looked puzzled and flustered. The media are never early to board meetings.

"The meeting doesn't start for 30 minutes," she explained.

I was trying to pay attention to her, but I was distracted. The clerk had begun preparing the sign-up sheet.

"I know," I replied. My eyes stayed fixed on the clerk. A few people began to gather around the sheet. My nerves kicked in.

"Is that where I sign up for public comment?" I pointed to the front desk.

She turned. "There? Yes." She paused, "Why?"

"I'm sorry," I said. "I need to get in line."

"Chris," she stepped in front of me. "Are you signing up for public comment?"

I didn't answer.

"Public comment is not for the media." Her voice cracked as she followed me to the forming line. "It's for parents and members of the community."

I watched the first speaker sign up.

"I know." I let the uncomfortable silence play out. Everyone in the atrium stood quiet, listening to our conversation.

"I've been trying to get an interview with the CEO or a board member. You won't speak with me," I explained.

Without a reply, she turned and fast-walked back to the elevator.

Now, everyone in the atrium was just staring at me.

I looked around at their peering eyes. "I've never done this before," I chuckled. "Can someone help me?"

An older woman behind me stepped forward, "It's easy. You just put your name, address and information here." She pointed at the sheet.

"How many people get to speak?" I asked.

"There are ten spots. You'll be fine," she replied. "We never have ten people sign up, anyway."

My name was fourth on the list.

This was just the second time in my career that I had signed up to comment at a public meeting. For journalists, this is a last resort. Our job is to guide the audience through a story. We never want to "be" the story. But I honestly felt I had no other choice.

Board meetings in Baltimore City are pretty standard. They start with the "Pledge of Allegiance," where most attendees still say, "under God." The minutes of previous meetings are then approved, and the Board discusses new business.

However, one unique aspect of Baltimore School Board meetings is that many feature a moment of silence to remember deceased students, many of whom were murdered. Their names are read along with a short biography highlighting their character and achievements.

For anyone familiar with Baltimore City board meetings, remembering murdered students is just part of the process. It's normal. For anyone new to board meetings, trust me, it's a shock to the system the first time you witness it.

Once the board meeting officially began, I positioned myself in the middle of the room. My cameraman set up on my left. Our producer sat to my right with a second camera. The boardroom itself is not nearly as fancy as the building. It's just a dark, square room with student art hanging on the walls. The board members' desks are arranged in a U-shape facing the audience.

Board meetings all follow a protocol. Public comment begins sharply at 6:30. Each speaker gets three minutes. Around 6:45, my name was called.

"Next guest, Chris Papst," the Board Chair announced.

I quickly glanced at our photographer to make sure he was ready. I then stood up and walked to the table facing the dais. The room was eerily quiet. Without a sound, I pulled the chair, sat down, and leaned into the mic.

"Good evening, Board Chair and Dr. Santelises. I came here tonight because I felt like I didn't have any other choice." Behind the dais, two large monitors began counting down from three minutes. There was no time to waste. I got right into it.

"This school board, and Dr. Santelises, is constantly saying that City Schools does not have enough money. Can you explain why you did not release the documents when we requested them? That decision cost taxpayers nearly $200,000."

I then cited the judge's ruling that City Schools "willfully and knowingly" violated the law to "hide possible wrongdoing."

"I believe taxpayers have a right to know who made that decision to violate the law, according to the judge. Has that person or have those people been held accountable?" I continued.

"Grade changing is happening at Baltimore City Public Schools. Those are the documents you did not want us to have and did not want us to read. We now have them as a result of this lawsuit. Your own investigator said grade changing is happening. What is this school board doing to address those concerns?"

As I spoke, nine school board members (all appointed by the mayor) and the CEO sat before me. Every year, they make billion-dollar decisions that affect tens of thousands of city students. The questions I asked were not hard. They all knew the answers. But when I finished, no one responded.

"No answers?" I asked as my three minutes expired.

The board chair responded, "Not right now."

"We will continue to reference you to the statements we made in the past," said Dr. Santelises. "You can submit, Mr. Papst. You are more than free to continue to submit your questions. Thank you."

After the meeting, I submitted the questions in writing that I had asked in person. North Avenue replied with this statement:

"City Schools is a public agency and, as we have indicated previously, we agree that the public should be kept informed about the district's activities. We also have responsibilities and legal obligations to protect the privacy of our students and families and to maintain the confidentiality of staff records. As we've also indicated previously, we believe that if staff and other members of our community are not confident we can protect their privacy, they will be less likely to alert us to potential improper activity and less candid during the course of investigations. This chilling effect will impede our ability to determine whether illegal or inappropriate activity has occurred and to take legal or disciplinary action when warranted.

Because of the seriousness of these concerns, we chose to defend our position in court. Unfortunately, the judge's ruling was not in our favor. As you know, as a result of the ruling, we have so far provided Fox45 News with more than 30,000 pages of documents that meet the broad scope of the judge's order, and our legal office is continuing to review material to prepare for release. We have nothing further to add at this time."

* * *

City Schools did all it could publicly to downplay the lawsuit and the subsequent release of its internal investigations. And Fox45 didn't get any assistance from the other television stations in the market.

Think about this for a minute. Baltimore City Public Schools is being sued for violating Maryland's public records law. A judge ruled that the school system intentionally broke the law by not releasing the documents. That judge monetarily reprimands the district to the tune of nearly $200,000. Then, once City Schools begins to release the documents, it shows "rounding up" failing grades to passing is an "unwritten practice" throughout the city. There are four television stations in the Baltimore market that produce local news, and to my knowledge, only Fox45 covered it. Let that sink in.

Television news is a highly competitive industry. When a city only has four television stations that produce local news, it's a constant battle for viewership. Most reporters, photographers and producers enjoy the competition. We thrive on it. It makes us better. But that spirit of competition doesn't always benefit the public to the degree it should. When the other three Baltimore stations ignored this situation, the public was underserved. If the other stations in the market had covered this story, additional pressure would have been placed on the school system to better address the systemic problems that lead to students being undereducated.

The *Baltimore Sun*, the paper of record in Maryland, also did not cover the story, to my knowledge. Most people in television news do not consider newspapers "competition" in the conventional sense. But maybe the Sun considered us competition, because they didn't touch this story as it played out over the years. Most U.S. cities only have one newspaper left. And they have influence. If the Sun, which is now under new ownership, had reported on this situation, along with the TV stations, additional pressure would have been placed on the school system to respond. How do I know this? Because it happened on the radio.

Many talk show hosts in the Baltimore area jumped on the story. Liberals and conservatives took umbrage with how City Schools acted. The reasoning behind their angst and their recommended solutions was rooted in different belief systems. But local radio talk show hosts wanted answers. And they wanted to hear those answers from City Schools' CEO. And one show got her to respond.

For 23 years, Larry Young served in Maryland's General Assembly. First as a delegate, then a senator. For 25 years following his public service, he hosted a morning radio show on WOLB Talk 1010 in Baltimore. He retired in 2022.

In 2019, when Project Baltimore began reporting on the results of our lawsuit, Young's show was all over it. WOLB has a largely African American audience centered in the city.

"You know, Larry, this is something . . . this is not good," said Young's co-host. "You talk about the foundation for our children. And right now, there's no transparency. No one wants to talk about it. No one is held accountable. So what are they doing? Who really cares about the children?"

Concerning our report on the principal who bought $30,000 worth of NBA tickets with school dollars, this was said on Young's show: "This is not the first time that there have been allegations and reports on misappropriation of funds at North Avenue and the schools. What is the most appalling is that people are trying to cover it up and sweep it under the rug, and not want the information to get out. I'm sure they could have found other ways and means to use that money other than buying $30,000 in Wizards tickets."

Young's co-host then declared, "I'm going to make sure that somebody comes on these airways, Larry, and explain their side of the story. Because this is ridiculous. I mean, this is ridiculous."

A short time later, following that challenge, Dr. Santelises appeared on Larry Young's show. Finally, for the first time, we heard from City Schools' leadership after we sued to get the public documents North Avenue didn't want the public to see.

"We are going to have a conversation," announced Young at the beginning of his broadcast. "Ladies and Gentlemen, Baltimore City Schools CEO Dr. Santelises."

As a journalist, I enjoy hearing other media personalities discuss my investigations. No matter their stance or opinion, it's affirming. But this was different. For years, I had been trying to speak with Dr. Santelises, and for years she declined every request. I appreciated Young using his platform to seek answers that the district refused to offer me.

"I was looking forward to this conversation for quite some time," Young stated to Santelises and his audience to start the broadcast.

Right away, Young called on Santelises to explain to parents and taxpayers why City Schools went to court with Fox45 over the release of internal grade-changing investigations. But even though Fox45 won the lawsuit nearly five months earlier, Santelises said she couldn't talk about it.

"That's right. And just because, you know, that with legal proceedings we need to be careful to protect the integrity of the legal proceedings," she said.

Santelises explained that the decision not to release the documents was made to protect whistleblowers, so they are not scared to come forward. This was the district's main talking point on the matter. But remember, in court, the judge completely dismissed that argument. So did Larry Young's co-host, Coach Butch McAdams.

"From my perspective, you could have done that without giving names," said McAdams. "The bigger picture here is the lack of transparency. And that particular entity had to go to court and sue, and they won."

The topic of holding school officials accountable was a main theme. But Santelises wouldn't say how anyone was disciplined for breaking the law.

"We did take disciplinary action where it was appropriate," she explained. "The challenge is that it's part of people's personnel files. And I think you can understand why we are not broadcasting people's personnel files in the public media."

McAdams wasn't buying any of it.

"Most of the stakeholders feel there is a lack of transparency," he fired back. "And when you have that, then people start to perceive, rightfully or wrongfully, that there is a cover-up. And that you are sweeping something under the rug."

Santelises responded, "In terms of sweeping anything under the rug. We've been very forthright. I've said why we initially redacted to the extent that the judge found unacceptable. After the judge ruled, we turned over the documents. We turned them over. We didn't appeal. We didn't do any of that. We said, 'Okay, the judge ruled,' and we released them."

"But you had to release them, other than appeal, that would have cost more money," McAdams' voice was rising with apparent frustration. Santelises was doing to him what the school system does to me.

"Coach, I would just say, look, the beauty of being in a country where we still have a court system is that there was a rationale to protect whistleblowers," continued Santelises. "The judge disagreed, and we complied. There is nothing illegal about doing that."

The fallout from this lawsuit was not over. Not even close. We were still waiting on more than 8,000 emails concerning grade changing that the judge ordered North Avenue to release. It would be another year-and-a-half before we'd get those emails. And the story they would tell would be explosive.

C H A P T E R   9

WHAT'S POSSIBLE

Since we had to wait a year and a half for City Schools to send us those emails, let's take a few chapters to discuss what's possible when it comes to public education.

Baltimore City Schools is a district that faces a number of challenges in educating kids, both inside and outside the classroom. Murder, crime, poverty, blight. It all takes a significant toll on children. But there are schools that have found ways to rise above the trauma.

There are about 160 individual schools spread throughout Baltimore. It works like this. Elementary students are zoned to a specific school. When a student enters middle school, they can choose where they go. If their first choice is full, the system defaults to their second choice. If their second choice is at capacity, they move to their third choice. Most schools have a lottery system. The higher performing schools in the city test students to determine who is eligible to enroll.

Since elementary schools are zoned, the students who attend must attend. Principals can't pick their students. So, when Project Baltimore heard about what was happening at Cecil Elementary in East Baltimore, we knew it was an inspiring story that had to be told. Cecil Elementary is a Maryland Blue Ribbon school in one of the most depressed parts of Baltimore. That alone is newsworthy, but I wanted to know *how* this school achieved success.

I'll never forget when I first spoke with Principal Roxanne Forr because, looking back, it told me all I needed to know about her.

First off, Forr was hard to reach. And what I mean by that is I would call her, leave a message, and never hear back. When she finally answered one of my calls, I was excited. She, however, could not have been less interested.

"Ms. Forr," I began, "thank you for taking my call. We are looking to profile your school for an upcoming Project Baltimore story."

"Why?" This was all she said.

That was not the response I expected. I could hear her typing frantically. I was clearly not her focus.

"I looked up the data on your school, and it's really impressive," I explained. "Your test scores are significantly higher than the elementary schools around you."

No reply. Just typing.

"We'd like to come to your school and follow you around for a day. You're clearly doing something different at Cecil Elementary. We'd like to find out what that is and share it with our viewers."

The typing never stopped. "I'm not doing anything different," she spoke quickly with no inflection.

"The numbers suggest otherwise," I said. "Ms. Forr, your school has a success story. We'd like to tell it."

"Listen," she snapped, "I don't have time to talk on the phone. If you want to come to my school, fine. I get here at 5:00 in the morning. Meet me tomorrow."

Again, not a response I expected. "Do you want me to contact North Avenue first? Get permission?"

I could hear her smile, "I usually don't."

"What about parental . . . ?"

She cut me off. The typing stopped.

"I know my kids. I know the ones you can record." I heard the springs of her chair release as she stood up. "Are we done?"

I was afraid to ask another question. "I believe so."

"Good. See you tomorrow morning."

The line went dead.

* * *

My photographer and I arrived at Cecil Elementary at 4:45 the following morning. We got there a little early. To be honest, I was scared to be late. She may not let us in.

Located near the intersection of Cecil Avenue and East 20th Street, the school is in a tough part of town. It's indistinguishable from the roughest parts of Baltimore. The block is cluttered with abandoned homes and spray-painted plywood windows. Knee-high grass split most every joint in the crumbling sidewalk. Some streetlights worked. Some didn't.

Then, all of a sudden, within the darkness, sat Cecil Elementary. Colorfully painted brick, with no broken windows or graffiti. The trees and patches of grass out front were healthy and trimmed. Little yellow footprints guided visitors down the sidewalk towards two bright blue doors.

When we pulled up, there was just one car sitting outside the school.

"I'm usually here by 5:00," Principal Forr said as she opened the door for us to enter. "I got here a little early today."

I had never been inside a school so early. It was eerily quiet. And eerily perfect.

"At 5:00 in the morning, I'm assuming you're the first person here?" I asked.

"Not always," she replied with a slight smile. "Sometimes the custodian is here before me."

Forr's demeanor was starkly different from the day prior. She was pleasant and welcoming. This was Roxanne Forr. Once students arrived, she became Principal Forr.

Cecil was a school Forr had shaped in her own image for 30 years. First, as a teacher. Then, as its principal. As we followed her around the school that day, she did the work of closing open lockers and picking up trash. She didn't walk the halls. She patrolled them.

If a student was in a hallway during class, she demanded to see his bathroom pass. I watched her tenderly address a crying student's needs while simultaneously enforcing the rules and expectations like a Marine drill sergeant. It was incredible to watch her work.

"Use your fork, where's your fork?" she barked at one student during lunch. He nearly wet himself while frantically searching the table for his fork.

She pointed, "Lips are closed until you show me how to use your utensils properly."

When one student stood up during lunch, her head snapped.

"Why are you up?" she roared—arm raised, palm out, with a finger pointed upward. "That's the first rule you broke, you know that."

The student immediately sat back down.

She then turned to a student loitering in the corner. "Why are you over here? Go get your lunch and get where you belong."

A slight white woman, Forr stood barely five feet tall—maybe 100 pounds after a big lunch. But I had never seen anyone demand such respect from children. Our camera did not impact the behavior. These students clearly respected her. Walking through that school, I got the impression they didn't necessarily fear her. Rather, they feared disappointing her.

"We get them at four. At four, they have a lot to learn, yet," she told me during our interview. "I'm not burned out now. Each day, you have to understand, with children, each day is so different."

But not all that different. With each student, each class and each generation that has passed through Cecil Elementary, there has always been one constant that has created this school's success.

"Ms. Forr put up with a lot, she put up with a lot with me," said one parent we spoke to. "My kids, like I said, that's my grandchild, my kids used to go here when they were small, so she know me and my whole family."

"Ms. Forr used to be my first-grade teacher, and she was also my third-grade teacher," said another parent of a child at the school.

I asked Forr about the benefit of having students whose parents she taught.

"So, when I call and ask for something," she smiled, "they are not going to say no to their first-grade teacher."

As I spent the day at Cecil, I learned Forr had crafted a bond that united this struggling community around its elementary school. Over the decades, when most chose to leave, Forr stayed.

"We know that the neighborhood can be a bit rough at times," said one parent whom we interviewed. "But we have Ms. Forr. That's why we're here."

How rough was this neighborhood? I pulled the numbers from Baltimore City Police. Within a half mile of Cecil, I counted thirteen robberies, ten thefts and three shootings, with eleven arrests made *that* week.

"We still come because we love Ms. Forr and we love the school," added another parent.

The reason parents love the school is the same reason why I initially called Forr and requested an interview. This school was special.

State data, at the time, showed 28 percent of students at Cecil Elementary were proficient in math. That number is up to nine times higher than nearby elementary schools that draw from the same neighborhoods, where upwards of 93 percent of children live in poverty.

English proficiency at Cecil is 26 percent. At nearby Dallas F. Nicholas Elementary, it's one percent. When we initially aired the story, these were the state proficiency percentages for the elementary schools nearest to Cecil. And keep in mind, Cecil Elementary gets the same funding as any other elementary school in the city.

	Math	English
Cecil	28	26
Harford Heights	3	2
Dallas F. Nicholas	5	1
Monarch	5	5
Dr. Bernard Harris	9	9

I asked Forr, "What makes this place different?"

"If I had the answer, I would definitely share it," she said honestly. "The longevity, I'm sure, has something to do with it."

Through the decades, as Ms. Forr decided to stay, others did too. Nearly half of Cecil's teachers (46%) had more than ten years of experience. At the elementary school down the road, three percent had more than ten years of experience.

"I think longevity builds some of those relationships, some of the openness, some of the trust that has to happen to move forward," stated Forr.

Forr spent a career building that trust with an honesty that doesn't stop when her students leave the building. Sometimes it shows up on a parent's doorstep.

"I hear rumors you walk kids home?" I asked.

"I do walk kids home when I need to," she smiled.

I follow up, "You go to the house to let them know you're not kidding? You're serious?"

"Absolutely," she proclaimed. "Just because you don't pick up a phone doesn't mean we're not in this together. It's that important."

It's important because this school has always been Forr's to shape. But she saw it as her students' to own.

A few hours after the dismissal bell rang and the teachers went home, Cecil Elementary returned to the same eerie quiet.

"I usually leave somewhere between five and six at night," Forr said to me.

I smiled, "You're the last person to leave?"

"No," she grinned. "Because the custodians are here."

I laughed. "Different custodians?"

"Yes, different custodians, but yes," she released a loud laugh that echoed through the empty school.

Principal Forr once again became Roxanne Forr.

A few weeks after we did that interview, Roxanne Forr was promoted to North Avenue as the Director of Leadership Support and Development. Soon after, following 35 years at Baltimore City Schools, she retired.

By 2024, three years after Forr retired, math proficiencies at Cecil Elementary had fallen to three percent. English proficiency fell to eight percent.

* * *

Success stories in City Schools are not limited to Cecil Elementary. The data suggests there are thousands of bright spots, via the students enrolled in full-day Pre-K. Around 2009, North Avenue experimented with the idea of full-day Pre-K as a way to better prepare students for kindergarten. And it seems to have worked. The data suggests that students in Baltimore Pre-K programs outperform every other grade level.

A student is considered ready for kindergarten if they have a certain amount of math, reading and language skills. Pre-K is designed to help develop those skills. But we found many of the gains that kids get from pre-K are lost when they enter elementary school in Baltimore City. And that has some saying that full-day Pre-K, while successful in its mission, is a waste of money.

If you were to visit any American Pre-K class, you're likely to see many of the same things. Things like insects. The parts of a bug. Head, thorax, abdomen. It's a common lesson taught to four-year-olds. The walls of Pre-K classes focus on phonics, numbers, colors, the alphabet, etc. Within the walls, young students full of energy want to learn.

The data over the past decade is similar. Let's look at 2022, for example. That year, 25 percent of students in Baltimore City who started kindergarten were considered ready to learn. Some would consider that the kindergarten equivalent to being proficient. But the data also suggests those gains are quickly lost. By third grade, those same students begin falling behind, and most never catch up. In that same year, 2022, 17 percent of elementary students were tested proficient in math. English Language Arts was 18 percent.

Between kindergarten and third-fifth grade, students lost about 30 percent in the proficiency levels.

In 2017, before she largely quit talking to me, I asked CEO Dr. Sonja Santelises what happens between kindergarten and third grade in that first round of state testing.

"That is a great question," she replied. "I know that data you cited and what it's doing is forcing us to look deeply to decide how we prioritize this work. We have a trajectory of success. We need to continue it."

In 2022, five years later, City Schools spent $39 million a year for about 2,700 students to attend Pre-K and early learning programs. But if the gains are lost by third grade, why spend those millions? Many argue that the money is wasted if the gains vanish. Opponents of full-day Pre-K say the money should be diverted elsewhere.

Dr. Santelises says the answer is not to trim the program to save money, but to find ways to build on the student gains.

"What we are doing now is taking a look at what we are doing in kindergarten, first," said Santelises. "If we don't capitalize on that early gain, young people will slide."

Which, they have. According to City Schools board-approved budgets, in 2017, the district spent about $6,800 per student in Pre-K. In 2024, that amount ballooned to about $13,000. According to City Schools online data, in 2017, 38 percent of city kindergarten students demonstrated readiness. In 2024, 39 percent demonstrated readiness. Taxpayers spent nearly double the amount of money for nearly identical results. Does that seem like a good investment?

* * *

The success of Baltimore's youngest students is not limited to City Schools Pre-K classes. There are other examples in the city where early education programs work. The problem still persists, however, that once the students get into public elementary school, their progress stalls or regresses. But rare instances of success show what is possible.

Reverend Al Hathaway is small in stature, soft in voice and calm in demeanor. But when he speaks, people listen. Hathaway possesses a unique wisdom, shaped by living and working in a depressed part of Baltimore for eight decades.

Keep that in mind as you read this report we produced on Hathaway and his school. The below script appears in its original form.

((START SCRIPT))

((ANCHOR))

Getting our kids off to the right start—the work often begins before they ever enter kindergarten.

((ANCHOR))

Project Baltimore Lead Investigative Reporter Chris Papst tells us how the program at Union Baptist recently did something no other Head Start in the city has ever done.

((TAKE PACKAGE))

West Baltimore . . .

Rev. Hathaway: "I spent my first seven years on this block."

. . . 1211 Druid Hill Avenue

Rev. Hathaway: "That was the address in which I was born."

In this area of the city, it's easy to just see the decades-old remnants of violence and vacancy. Reverend Al Hathaway of Union Baptist Church sees something different.

Rev. Hathaway: "Here I am now, a son of this church, now the pastor of this church. Now, the head of our Head Start program, right at the address in which I was born."

His childhood home—now home to 175 children Monday through Friday at the city's oldest, and perhaps most successful, Head Start.

Rev. Hathaway: "I affirm them, to make certain that they know there's an environment where they're loved and respected."

Head Start is an early education program for three and four-year-olds in low-income areas. The idea started in the 1960s as part of the War on Poverty. The program at Union Baptist also started in the 60s. And last year, it did something no other Head Start in Baltimore has ever done: it received five stars from the Maryland State Department of Education, its highest rating. Every other Head Start in the city has a three or fewer.

Gayle E. Headen: "I remember when I first came here, I used to, when I was blessing my food, thank God every day for allowing me to be here. And I still feel that way 15 years later."

Gayle Headen is just the third director in this Head Start's 52-year history. And she understands what this program means to this community because in 1970, when she was three, she went here.

Papst Question: "Do you think about what you're doing here in an area of West Baltimore that many people have just kind of dismissed?"

Gayle E. Headen: "Yes. Do we think about it? Yes, and we think about it every day, and that's why we know what we do is so important."

Now, with nearly 200 students, Union Baptist Head Start runs at capacity. The wait list to get in is a full year. Kids who go here don't just learn their ABCs, they receive social, emotional, health and nutritional services through community partnerships, like the Breathe Bus for students suffering from asthma.

Gayle E. Headen: "Yes, we are preparing them for school, but for beyond that. We're preparing them for so much more. It's a wonderful place to be. It is . . . it brings purpose to my life every day. And I know . . . I know that what I do and what we do makes a difference."

A difference, generations in the making.

Rev. Hathaway: "Now I can make certain that doors are open for young people in this community, just like they were open for me. We're going to make certain that we expose our children to the best that we have to make them successful."

((END SCRIPT))

* * *

Getting to know Reverend Hathaway was an honor. And he is fully aware of the regression that takes place when his students enter the public school system. He is also aware that when he was growing up, 70 years earlier, he felt he received a quality education from the Baltimore City Public School system.

After our interview, when the photographers were breaking down their cameras and lights, I asked him, "What happened? Why do you think you received a good education from this school system, and today most students do not?"

With experienced eyes, he peered through thick glasses, "My honest opinion." He paused, "The teachers' union."

I remained quiet, awaiting an explanation. My father was a teacher and in a union for 35 years in Pennsylvania. I never saw the union as a destructive educational force. Growing up, I saw the teachers' union as an entity that helped my father do his job and, therefore, helped our family.

"When I was in school," Hathaway explained, "there was no union. They didn't get popular until the early '70s. Prior to that, being a teacher was a profession, no different than a doctor or a lawyer. It was a profession."

He had my attention.

"When the union got involved, teaching became a job." He used the chopping of an open hand to emphasize his point. "*This* is when you start in the morning. *This* is when you eat lunch. *This* is when you get a break. *This* is what you teach. *This* is how you teach it. *This* will be your pay. *This* will be your pay ten years from now. *This* is when you go home."

He wasn't explaining this in a malicious way. He wasn't denigrating unions. There was no angst in his voice. I just got the impression he was answering my question in the sincerest way he could.

"When being a teacher went from a profession to a job," he lowered his head. "That is when everything changed."

* * *

By now, you've probably realized I like data. I enjoy analyzing random sets of numbers. Where most people see unorganized confusion, I see potential news stories. Such was the case when I randomly pulled Maryland's school poverty data. Every public school has a poverty index, which influences the amount of funding the school receives. Sitting in my office one day, I was paging through spreadsheets of poverty data for every school in Maryland. At the time, I was looking for something specific. But I stumbled upon something remarkable.

When I saw it, I immediately called the school.

My initial conversation with Principal Thomas Garner was similar to Roxanne Forr. He didn't understand why I wanted to interview him.

"I don't think we're doing anything special here," he told me during our initial conversation.

"The numbers tell me you are," I replied.

A few days later, the Project Baltimore team drove 90 minutes west to Salem Avenue Elementary in Hagerstown, Maryland.

We arrived at the school during morning drop-off. Buses, parents, teachers, staff—it was loud and hectic.

When we got out of the car, I didn't know who Principal Garner was. We had only spoken on the phone. Small in stature, with short brown hair and glasses, he doesn't stand out in a crowd. But his presence was obvious, standing outside his school. In a Salem Avenue Elementary T-shirt, he was greeting every student as they arrived. He knew all their names. And they knew his.

"Excuse me," I said to a parent in the parking lot. "Does he do this every day?"

She affirmed. "And at pick-up."

Salem Avenue looked like any other red-brick quasi-suburban school in America. It wasn't old. It wasn't new. But it was clean and well-kempt.

We scheduled the interview during picture day. Inside, for most of the morning, single-file lines of behaved students stretched down every hallway. On this day, 750 elementary school kids would say, "cheeeeese." And within all of those smiles, Principal Garner saw potential.

"We expect all kids to be able to do well. Period." He told me.

In his nearly two decades at this Hagerstown school, Garner had learned to set his expectations high and his threshold for excuses low.

"I don't want there to be reasons why kids can't be successful. As a principal, my job can't be to let the outside forces control what happens within our building."

Those "outside forces" comprised half the reason we chose to interview Principal Garner. As I was analyzing that statewide school poverty data, I noticed something interesting. Maryland has about 1,400 schools. At the time, two had 100% student poverty. Salem Avenue Elementary was one of them. This school was the poorest school in Maryland. Every single student lived in poverty.

"You have to be aware of it," I said to Garner during our interview. "But what do you think about it?"

He lightly smiled and tilted his head, "We're completely aware of it. It is in our environment. My job is to show empathy, to be empathetic from where you're coming from, but my job is also to push you up, to move you up."

Hagerstown, Maryland, is a blue-collar town of some 40,000 people. Overall, it has a higher poverty rate than Baltimore City. Its small-town charm has been overshadowed by a major public health crisis. The city sits at the intersection of Interstates 70 and 81, locally known as the "Heroin Highway."

"We're dealing with kids who sometimes are seeing a lot of trauma at home," Garner explained with compassion. "And sometimes they are actually helping bring their parents back. Maybe in the middle of the night, they're delivering Narcan to bring their own parent back."

Over time, Garner watched as America's opioid epidemic severely impacted his school. In just a few short years, Salem Avenue Elementary went from 64 percent poverty to 100 percent. Every student at the school receives free breakfast and lunch, which are often their only meals of the day.

As the community around the school deteriorated, Garner knew he had to do something. So, he came up with an idea to strengthen the connection between his school and his families. He called it "The Blitz."

"You can't really walk in someone's shoes until you've kind of walked in their shoes," he told me.

Every year, on the day before school starts, Garner passes out T-shirts and maps to his entire staff. The T-shirts say, "The 1323 is the place to be." The school address is 1323. The maps supply the addresses for every student at the school. In one day, every teacher at Salem Avenue visits all of their students' homes.

"A lot of them don't have anything," said math teacher, Tyler Newcomer, who was on the first blitz and every one since. "I mean, I have had kids with no electricity, with no running water. And that's common."

"It's tough," he explained. "It's difficult to know that this is what our kids go home to. For a large majority of our kids, this school is the best thing they have."

Newcomer says seeing where his students come from has made him a better teacher. He doesn't give homework. He's seen what's at home. But knowing his students have little, doesn't mean he expects less.

"We have very high expectations, and it starts with respecting our kids and teaching them that they can do it," Newcomer explained.

Salem Avenue is a Title I school, meaning it gets extra federal funding to help low-income students. Maryland has about 400 Title I schools. At

Salem, any extra money goes towards books, which nowadays may be rare. But Garner says it's important and has helped set his school apart.

"Are you aware of your test scores?" I asked Garner during our interview.

His expression didn't change. "I am."

And those test scores comprise the other reason we chose to interview Principal Garner.

Despite every student at Salem Avenue living in poverty, the fifth-grade class scored higher on state proficiency tests than the Maryland average.

	English	Math
Salem Avenue 5th grade	42.3%	38.4%
Maryland 5th grade	42.2%	38.0%

The other grades weren't far behind the state average. This was not a story about a school where every student lives in poverty. This was a story about students who outperformed more than half their state peers, when conventional wisdom says they shouldn't.

"I don't want there to be reasons why kids can't be successful," Garner told me. "It's too easy to say, 'this happened last night' or 'that happened last night.'"

"The kids don't know that they're in the poorest school in the state of Maryland," said Newcomer with tears in his eyes. "That's out of their control."

He paused to curb his emotions and gather his true thoughts, "We love our kids. We have the best kids."

Former Baltimore City Schools barbering teacher, Marvin Lee. "These kids aren't failing because they can't do it. They're failing because they know they can, that's the difference."

Calverton Elementary/Middle as it appeared in 2017. The school has since been demolished.

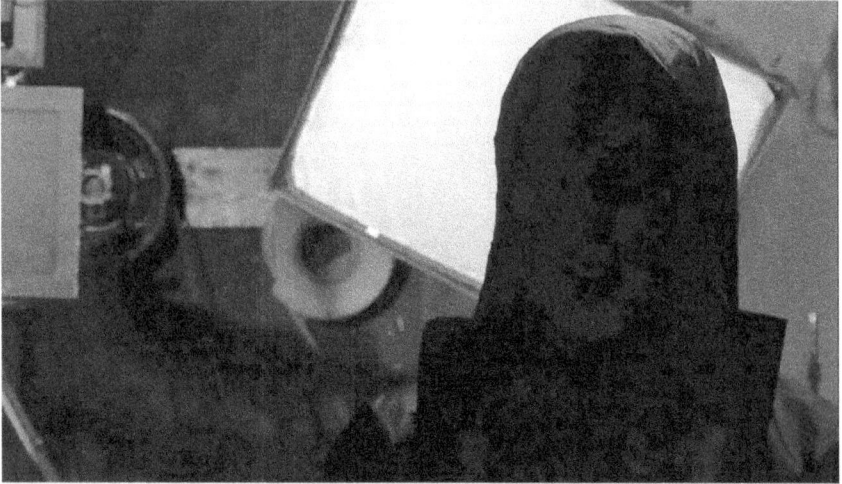

Calverton Elementary/Middle teacher. One of the initial employees who blew the whistle on widespread grade changing in Baltimore City Schools.

An employee yelling, "No comment," from behind the locked door of a school accused of grade changing. I replied, "You don't even know what my questions are, how can you say, 'no comment?'"

City Schools Board of Education Chair Cheryl Casciani (left) and CEO Dr. Sonja Santelises (right) watch as I address the school board during public comment.

Ciara Ford and her son outside their West Baltimore home. Ford was upset that her son, who was absent or late 147 days that school year, still passed to the next grade.

Two Baltimore City Schools police officers prevent me from speaking with Calverton's principal, who had been accused of grade changing. Allegations that were later substantiated.

Our attorney and I entering court for the first time after Fox45 sued Baltimore City Schools for violating Maryland's Public Information Act.

Roxanne Forr, principal of Cecil Elementary, scolds a child who dares to challenge her authority during lunch.

Principal Thomas Garner's school, Salem Avenue Elementary, academically outperforms most schools in Maryland, despite 100% of its students living in poverty.

> **FORMER AUGUSTA FELLS STUDENT**
>> LISTED AMONG 21 APPARENT GHOST STUDENTS

This "Ghost Student" dropped out of Baltimore Schools after he was incarcerated. Yet, someone enrolled him in school, where taxpayers paid to educate him, even though he was in jail.

Gregory Gray explains how Baltimore City Schools failed to properly educate his son. "They passed them, they just passed them along. He didn't know the material."

Maryland's Governor (left) and Lieutenant Governor (right) respond to my reporting on City Schools' failures. "It's because of incompetence and mismanagement and complete lack of accountability and the wasting of money."

An irate former teacher, Aaron Thompson, bashes City Schools for passing students who did not earn it. "You think social promotion doesn't have a long-term impact on their life trajectory?"

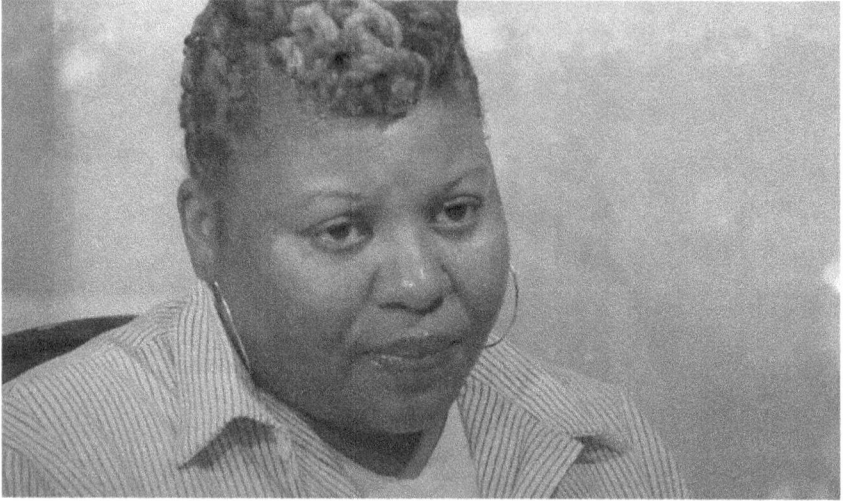

A high school dropout, Michelle Bradley, explains how City Schools promoted her through the grade levels even though she never learned how to read.

The "school" in East Baltimore, where students could get a state-certified high school diploma in two hours.

This is 200 East North Avenue – Baltimore City Public Schools headquarters. By far, the nicest building on the street.

My photographer and I chasing Dogwood Elementary's principal through the parking lot. She refused to answer questions about an apparent cover-up of violence at her school.

Me speaking during public comment at a Baltimore City School Board meeting. "Grade changing is happening. Those are the documents you did not want us to have."

Radio talk show hosts Clarence Mitchell IV (left) and Larry Young (right). I commend both men for picking up our reporting and trying to hold school officials accountable.

The bullying at Reality Adams' school was so bad, she tried to take her own life. Her family says administrators ignored the violence to protect the school's reputation.

Rianna Facey and her mom sit on the front steps of their Baltimore home as the nine-year-old reads her book The Cat That Wouldn't Go Away.

This student missed 110 school days in his senior year. Yet, he still walked across the stage during graduation. "I can say some people who graduated shouldn't have graduated."

Tiffany France pleads for help after learning her son, who had been in high school for four years, was still a freshman.

CHAPTER 10

WHAT ELSE IS POSSIBLE

As a member of the media, I often hear the following: "Why don't you cover more good news?" It's a legitimate question rooted in legitimate concern. Media narratives are powerful, and visuals are influential. People care about their communities, and they want to hear positive messages to reinforce why they chose to live in their specific state, county or neighborhood. I'm the same way. I think we all are.

But "good news" and "bad news" are not objective. If a city's mayor is found guilty of a crime and goes to jail, some may view that as "bad news" because it makes their city look corrupt. But others could consider it "good news" because it demonstrates accountability in government.

Either way, when I'm asked the question, "Why don't you cover more good news?" I usually answer this way—I define news as the absence of normalcy. What is not normal is newsworthy. If so-called "good news" becomes so rare that it regularly grabs headlines, your community is in trouble. If so-called "bad news" becomes so pervasive that it becomes normal, and is therefore no longer newsworthy, your community is in even more trouble.

Throughout my career, I've always gauged potential reports by combining community impact with relative frequency. If a public high school graduates around 85 percent of its students every year, that school is normal. That school will not appear in the news. Essentially, that school and its students did their jobs. And someone simply doing their job should not be newsworthy.

But if that school begins to deviate from the norm, in either direction, it begins to become newsworthy. With greater deviation comes a greater number of students, parents and taxpayers impacted. At some point, whether that school inches towards 100 percent or zero percent graduation, it becomes increasingly newsworthy. The absence of normalcy.

But what if there were a school that offered students a chance to earn a diploma, certified by the Maryland State Department of Education, after just a few hours of class work? Tuition is set at around a few hundred bucks. And almost every student who enrolls gets a diploma. Would that be newsworthy? Would you consider that a positive or negative story? Either way, in a city like Baltimore, it shows what else is possible.

I was sitting at my desk at work when this email appeared in my mailbox:

> Hi Mr. Papst: Just a concerned Baltimore resident & professional
> trainer and advocate for "Doing the right thing" & being the
> change I want to see in the world. I work for a non-profit organiza-
> tion that does specialized training. I assist individuals with finding
> employment and I have met some people who have obtained a HS
> Diploma from what I think may be a fraudulent business . . . mean-
> ing I don't think people are really getting the information/education
> needed to obtain a HS diploma. I have attached a copy of one of
> the HS Diploma's . . . I guess my concern is that people are paying
> money to get a HS Diploma, but are not being afforded the proper
> education/training to support it and it makes things 100x's more
> difficult for community providers to assist individuals with finding
> employment if they do not have basic skills needed.
>
> Andrea Harrison
> "Be the CHANGE you wish to see in the WORLD"—Gandhi

Here is a copy of the diploma attached to the email.

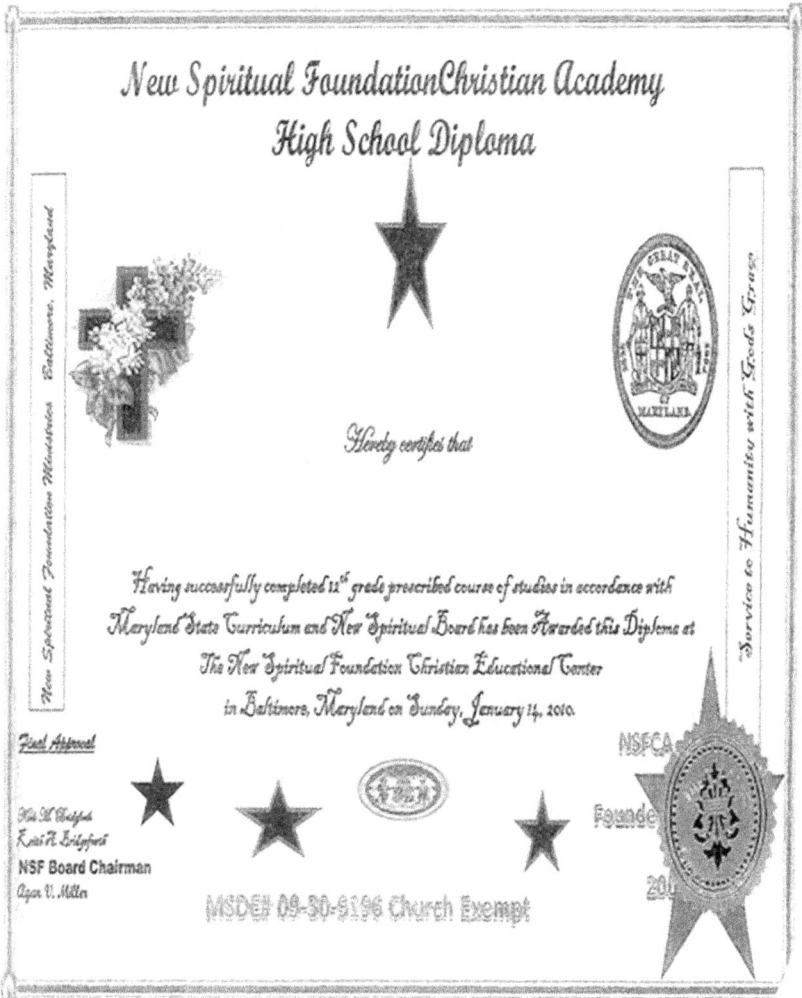

The diploma certainly appeared unique. Yet strangely official. It even had a raised seal on the bottom right. I wasn't sure what to make of it, which piqued my journalistic interest. That day, I called Andrea and set up an interview. At first, I wasn't sure if this was even a story. Seven months later, this investigation would take us to Virginia, Ohio and right to the leadership of the Maryland State Assembly.

"I was like, 'Is this a real high school diploma from Maryland?'" stated Harrison during our interview.

Harrison, as she explained in her email, was a former caseworker who helped city residents find jobs. Harrison was about 40 years old, with dark skin and high, tight hair. Through a soft voice, she emitted a strong confidence.

A few years before she contacted Project Baltimore, Harrison started seeing clients with this new type of high school diploma, and something didn't seem right.

"I would say their reading level was very low, and people were struggling with basic words. So, that's a problem," explained Harrison. "I think this high school diploma is fraudulent. I wouldn't say that to the person, but I would think it."

The diploma, as you can see on the previous page, is issued by New Spiritual Foundation Christian Academy. It features the Great Seal of Maryland and states the student has completed the "Maryland State Curriculum." If nothing else, I was certainly intrigued by this diploma. So, we began to look into it.

Here's what we found. New Spiritual is what's known as a church-exempt school. What's that? It comes from an old state law that allows religious institutions to set up private schools. There are around 500 in Maryland. Many are supported by large churches. New Spiritual, on the other hand, was located on the second floor of a run-down row home on East Federal Street in Baltimore.

When we reached out to the school's founder, he agreed to an interview.

"We get individuals who have been thrown out of six schools. Basically, the system has no more place for that individual." Kirk Bridgeforth founded New Spiritual Foundation Christian Academy in 2006. "There is a need for what we provide."

Like Harrison, Bridgeforth appeared to be in his 40s. He was average height, a little heavy, and bald. Though unlike Harrison, Bridgeforth was not soft-spoken.

New Spiritual's website promoted a quality education. It featured pictures of happy graduates. Videos highlighted a "Curriculum for Excellence." Its accreditation was highly touted. An Ohio State University professor even received a "special thanks" on the website for inspiring the school. Tuition to attend—less than $200.

"Our goal is to prepare our students to be able to function in their freshman year on any college campus," Bridgeforth told me. "We give them an atmosphere to find themselves, and that's what I've been looking for all my life is to teach in an environment where students are free."

This story, at first glance, could have been about high school dropouts working hard and overcoming adversity to earn high school diplomas. This story, at first glance, could have been about a man who devoted his life to providing an affordable, quality education to an underserved community. That is certainly how Bridgeforth sold it. And it sounded good. Almost too good.

Unfortunately for Bridgforth, Project Baltimore kept digging. Turns out church-exempt schools don't get much oversight. In fact, the State Department of Education, which certifies them, according to its own records, had never visited New Spiritual.

"If there is no one checking the credentials, the credibility, that's disheartening, to say the least," responded Harrison when we told her what we found concerning the diploma she gave us.

In a statement to Fox45, the Maryland Department of Education said, "Church-exempt schools fall under the guidance of their sponsoring church organizations and, as such, are exempt under the State law from the oversight of the State Board."

Okay, but if the state had checked New Spiritual, here's what it would have found. On one of the school's websites, former students called the school a "scam" and the diploma "fake." One person says they got a lawyer because their "diploma was a phony." Why? Because the diploma is not accepted at local colleges and universities.

Remember that Curriculum for Excellence video on the school's website? We traced that video back to a post on the Scottish government's YouTube channel. As for that OSU professor prominently featured on the website, we called him. He said he gave New Spiritual permission to use his name, but he knows very little about the school.

And then there's that highly touted accreditation? It's from the Faith-Based Christian Services of Maryland.

"We sat down and talked about what standards should be met for a Christian education," said Bridgeforth during our interview when I asked him about his school's accreditation.

The CEO of Faith-Based was Tiffany Outerbridge, who we learned is also a founding member of New Spiritual.

I asked Bridgeforth if that's a conflict of interest.

"No," he replied.

I followed up, ". . . that a founder accredits the school?"

"No." That was all he said.

Accreditation is vital to a school. But we couldn't find anything about Faith-Based online. No website. No social media. No business registration. It's like it didn't exist. So, I asked Bridgeforth where it's located.

He told me, "Baltimore."

The problem with that answer is that it's not factually correct. We were able to track down Faith-Based, but it's not in Maryland. An address on New Spiritual's website eventually led us to an apartment in a housing complex in Newport News, Virginia.

At this point in our interview, Bridgeforth started to sweat. His voice grew louder. "There's a thing in this country called separation of church and state. I think it applies here."

Bridgeforth was not a bad guy. I think he was sincerely trying to help the undereducated. And in a city like Baltimore, there are generations of high school dropouts who create a market for what Bridgeforth was offering—a cheap, fast and easy high school diploma. The failures of the public school system allowed New Spiritual to fill a need. And he did so by operating under a religious statute set forth by the State Department of Education that certifies all church-exempt high school diplomas in Maryland.

Bridgeforth knew what he was doing. And I knew what I was doing, which meant I needed to be careful. I didn't want any problems. But his school was charging people hundreds of dollars, and accepting taxpayer dollars (we'll get to this later) while issuing what equated to a piece of paper with some words on it.

"It's an empty promise," Harrison told Fox45. "If there's no oversight to protect the students, the system's broken. I've had teenagers, 18, 20, 30, 40-year-olds with this diploma. Something has to be done. We can't . . . I disagree with it not being any type of checks and balances. It doesn't make sense."

Harrison was right. It didn't seem to make sense. This whole situation didn't make sense. We needed more information. The unknowns were simply too alluring. So, we sent a guy inside.

We asked an employee at Fox45 if he would be willing to enroll as a student at New Spiritual, take the classes, and do the work necessary to graduate. We wanted to know how long it would take to earn a diploma and at what level of effort. Our "student" jumped on board immediately.

In Maryland, you cannot record someone's audio without their consent. So, we fitted our "student" with undercover cameras that did not record audio and sent him in.

Whenever our "student" was inside New Spiritual, we were sitting in a car outside, just in case. We always parked facing away from the row home and watched via the rearview and sideview mirrors.

Our "student" was an actual student at Towson University. Through his undercover camera, we watched as he entered New Spiritual and walked up a dark stairwell into a small room cluttered with stacks of paper and exposed wires. There, he met the school's founder, Kirk Bridgeforth.

Our "student" gave Bridgeforth $180 to enroll in New Spiritual. In exchange, he got his first assignment—a 21-page work packet that covers some English, science and ends with math. Decimals, fractions and angles.

After receiving the packet, we picked him up down the street.

"Got your packet?" I asked as he got into the car.

He handed me a large manila envelope. "Got my packet."

"How'd it go?" I replied.

His response was immediate, "It was not what I expected. It was interesting."

Later that day, our "student" began working on his assignment. What challenged him the most was not the questions, but rather the mistakes.

He showed me many errors in the packet. One question asked students to be "*underling* words you do not know."

We believe the word should have been "underlining."

For another task, the packet suggested students should be "using a dictionaries." Instead of "dictionary."

"It almost makes me not want to finish this, honestly," our "student" said.

That first assignment turned out to be his only assignment. A few days later, he took his final exam at New Spiritual, passed and got this— his high school diploma.

"How long did it take you to fill out the packet?" I asked after he graduated.

"About an hour, give or take," he said.

"Okay," I replied. "How long did it take you to complete that test?"

He thought for a moment, "It took me about an hour and ten minutes to take the test, I believe."

I did some quick math. "So, it took you two hours and fifteen minutes to get your high school diploma?"

He nodded, "Around there, yes."

"And $180," I added.

He affirmed, "Yes. Half the stuff on the transcript. I didn't do half of that."

A two-hour diploma. We had some questions.

"Who are our students? Cast-offs from Baltimore City Schools," Bridgeforth told me during our interview.

At this point in our discussion, I told Bridgeforth we had been looking into New Spiritual. And then, I told him this. "We had somebody enroll in your school."

His powerful voice weakened, "Who is that?"

"I'm not going to give you his name," I stated.

According to our "student's" transcripts, he earned a 3.1 GPA—straight Bs. In his two hours, he apparently took a lot of classes, including film appreciation, Phys. Ed. and computer applications. Twenty-three credits total from four instructors—three he had never met.

"It took about two hours and fifteen minutes to get a diploma from your school," I said as I presented Bridgeforth with the transcripts we acquired from New Spiritual.

He quickly looked at them. "How do I know this is legit?"

"Are you saying this is not from your school?" I asked.

He replied, "It looks like our stuff."

That's because it is.

I started to read the classes from the transcript. "Chemistry II, Chemistry III. He got Bs in those. These classes are being taken in your school?"

Bridgeforth was getting nervous, "Yeah. Yeah."

I kept pressing him. "He got a B minus in essay writing. He didn't write an essay. Seventy-five service hours is the one that really stuck out to us because he didn't do any service hours."

"It's up to the student to get that," Bridgeforth explained.

I should have been stunned by that response. But I wasn't. "So, you just take their word for it?"

He avowed, "Yes."

"This is 9th grade. A 9th grader could probably do this. It looks extremely juvenile." We showed New Spiritual's work packet to Dianna Dinkins at the Druid Heights Community Development Center, which offers free GED classes in West Baltimore.

She was stunned and saddened.

"It looks like I could have just printed it out on my computer at home," said Dinkins. "This is, it's really unfortunate. I would say, give me those students in my class, please. I can help them for real, free of charge. Please."

Dinkins says schools like New Spiritual make her job harder while contributing to a large problem.

"It just does a disservice to our students and even our children, that I know, need the help, need the real help," she concluded.

* * *

Days after we ran our first stories on New Spiritual, the state suspended the school's church exempt status. The State Department of Education acted fast. They had to. In addition to raising questions about the value of its diploma, our seven-month-long investigation into New Spiritual also found safety concerns. The State Department of Education confirmed to Fox45, the reason New Spiritual's license was suspended was not because of the diplomas Bridgeforth issued, but rather due to the building from which he issued them.

"It's the first time I've heard of a situation like this. It's unbelievable." As the then-Chair of the Education subcommittee in Annapolis, few people knew more about Maryland schools than Delegate Erik Luedtke. But when he learned of our findings concerning New Spiritual, he was taken by surprise.

"I think your story is going to change the conversation. Start a new conversation about these programs," said Luedtke.

Over a five-year period, New Spiritual has been awarded $37,000 from the State Department of Education for materials, like textbooks and computers. But since the Department of Education had never visited New Spiritual, it had no clue how the money was actually being spent.

Also, the State doesn't even appear to check its *own* records before issuing tax dollars to church exempt schools. As it was handing tax dollars to New Spiritual, the school was "Not in Good Standing" with the State Tax Department. The business hadn't filed personal property returns in two years.

Another potential problem, state law requires church-exempt schools to be "operated by a bona fide church." We looked up New Spiritual tax records; it's not a non-profit church. In its twelve years, it's never been one.

"We haven't . . . Actually, we haven't even finished the application," Bridgeforth admitted when I asked about his non-profit status.

Since New Spiritual was a church-exempt school, we wondered: Where's the church? Maryland records filed by Bridgeforth show it was located on the second floor of a nondescript building in East Baltimore. A woman who claimed to be the property owner let us in. All we found was an empty room.

The property manager said she wasn't aware a church was renting from her. And she knew nothing about church services being held in the space.

Is it possible that people create fake churches, which are then used to establish schools that charge tuition, only to distribute worthless diplomas that are backed by the state?

As our investigation into Bridgeforth and his school continued, we did find New Spiritual's building permit for the row home on East Federal Street. The address was zoned as a single-family attached dwelling. This school is not approved by the city to be a school. This is important because there's no code enforcement. No safety checks. No sprinklers. No fire escapes.

When we learned about this, I had to challenge Bridgeforth. "You knew that you did not have the authority to operate a school, and for the past ten years, you've been operating a school at that location?"

"We've been there for ten years and we have been operating, and it hasn't been a problem," he replied. At this point in the interview, he was defending the indefensible, and he knew it.

"But you understand," I continued, "that there are safety codes that are involved in operating a business."

"I've had enough of this." Bridgeforth reached under his shirt and took off his mic. "Thank you for the interview."

In my career, I've had very few people walk out of an interview. My intent was not to pressure Bridgeforth into leaving. But there were questions we had to ask. If adults want to pay him for a worthless diploma, that is one thing. But he was cramming people into this "school" without regard for their safety. That is why the Maryland State Department of Education shut his school down. We had to press him on it.

"This is about an attempt to kill the program," he said after removing the mic. "And good luck."

Bridgeforth's demeanor seemed to conflict with itself. He appeared frustrated, but also angry and a little contrite. Then, in a sudden instant, that cocktail of emotions exploded.

"A lot!" He suddenly yelled. His voice boomed throughout the room. "It takes a lot! We have comedy shows three times a year just to raise money to keep the Goddamn building we got, the computers we have!" He then lowered his head, almost in shame. His voice lowered with it.

"Chief," he could no longer look at me. His eyes dropped. "We can't do it no better." Tears welled in his eyes. "Can't do it no better."

He then stood up. And walked out of the room.

We conducted the interview on the second floor of WBFF's studios in Baltimore. When he left, a security guard escorted him down the stairs and outside. It was a security guard we had requested to stand outside the room.

As a human, I felt bad for Bridgeforth. As a journalist, I had to do my job.

"Clearly, we can be doing better," said Delegate Luedtke after watching our story on New Spiritual. "We have consumer protections. So those same types of consumer protections should be provided for people who are going to non-public schools. Clearly, what this case brings out is that there isn't enough oversight. My preference would be, if we're going to have schools that have almost no regulation, we shouldn't be giving public money to them. That's absolutely something I would be willing to introduce legislation about."

The $37,000 issued to New Spiritual came through a state textbook and technology program. That program awards up to $6 million a year to non-public schools throughout Maryland. After New Spiritual's license was suspended, the state recovered some of the taxpayer-issued products offered to the school.

"I think that's a fundamental issue we need to address in the legislature," added Luedtke. "If this is happening with one school, then it begs the question, is it happening elsewhere?"

* * *

As this story continued to unfold, we interviewed one child in the foster care system who was sent to New Spiritual by the Department of Social Services. The state was sending foster kids to Bridgeforth's school. The student told us the diploma he got, which taxpayers paid for, was a lie.

"I just don't wanna walk around carrying a lie," said Geremiah Matthews, the foster child. He graduated from New Spiritual in three weeks.

"I just was like, 'I got my high school diploma. I'm gonna be somebody,'" he said, shaking his head in disappointment. At first, he believed the lie. His transcript from the school said he earned 23 credits with a 3.1 GPA. Some of the classes he took included Biology II, Biology III, Chemistry II and Chemistry III.

"Never been in chemistry," he said. "Never been in biology."

"Did the foster care system think it was weird that you got a high school diploma in three weeks?" I asked.

He shook his head, "Nobody said anything."

The diploma and the transcript cost $180. And who paid for it? State taxpayers. Geremiah says the Department of Social Services paid his tuition at New Spiritual. And this is not the first time DSS has come under scrutiny for similar payments.

In 2013, the *Baltimore Sun* reported that the Baltimore City Department of Social Services sent dozens of students to Philadelphia and paid $500 for each to take a test and get their high school diploma in one day.

Project Baltimore contacted the department, which declined an interview. But we were told the agency creates an educational plan for foster kids. Schools are identified using a vendor list. "Nonpublic schools are treated like all other vendors and are subject to the standard review process," explained the statement.

Since church-exempt schools are approved by the State Department of Education, New Spiritual was on the vendor list. After we did our stories, it was removed. But that year, BCDSS paid $67,621 for 507 city kids seventeen and older to attend these schools.

"I know it was a small amount of money, but money is money, period," said Geremiah. "So, if you're going to give out money, you should know at least where your money is going."

Matthews says, since DSS paid his tuition and since the State Department of Education certifies church-exempt schools, he assumed the education he was getting was the education he needed. He didn't realize that church-exempt schools receive no oversight once approved by the state. But he didn't get an education. He simply got a piece of paper that said he got an education.

"I feel like a victim," he lamented. "But I also feel like I should have took a closer look into it and not just have been so excited."

We also heard from an irate Baltimore County family, who says Baltimore County Public Schools—America's 24th largest school system—recommended their son attend New Spiritual Foundation Christian Academy to obtain a high school diploma. The teenager said his school counselor, someone who is supposed to be guiding him in the right direction, suggested he drop out of high school and enroll in New Spiritual.

"I'm angry. I'm angry," said Tamara Dunham. "I'm not one of those type of parents that expects the school system to take care of my child. But, at least have my child's best interest at heart, and they didn't."

Her son, Erick Dunham, was a senior at Lansdowne High School in Baltimore County when we spoke to them. But as graduation approached, Erick was in danger of failing. In late spring, his guidance counselor offered him and his mom another graduation option.

"She had said that she had sent kids there before, and they would come out with their diploma." Tamara said she trusted the school system with her son's educational future.

So, Erick dropped out of Lansdowne, paid $180, and enrolled in New Spiritual.

"They wanted to hurry up and transfer him out of the school system, so he was no longer a statistic, a negative statistic, on their reports." The mom never calmed down during our interview. She was really upset. She felt scammed.

Dunham's experience at New Spiritual was similar to other former students Fox45 interviewed, including the "student" we enrolled. He said he did about two hours of work, graduated and received a transcript full of classes he never took.

Erick gave me a copy of his transcripts. On camera, I read through the classes he apparently passed.

Papst: "U.S. history?"

Erick: "No."

Papst: "Social studies?"

Erick: "No."

Papst: "Film, social issues?"

Erick: "No. Double no."

Papst: "You took quantum theory?"

Erick: "No, I did not."

Papst: "You got a C in quantum theory, dark energy."

Erick: "No, I did not."

I also asked Erick about the row home.

"I didn't feel safe at all," he said. "It was a town home. When you stepped on the stairs, it creaked. It just felt really old."

Baltimore County Public Schools declined an interview with Fox45. At the time, BCPS received about $2.5 billion a year to educate 111,000 students. And it sent at least this one student to a school that didn't meet safety codes. Since they refused to interview with us, we sent an email to BCPS asking a series of questions:

- How many BCPS students have attended New Spiritual?
- Was BCPS aware that it was referring students to a school that did not meet safety codes?
- Does the Dunham family's story concern BCPS, or is this acceptable to the school system and its superintendent?

We heard nothing back. No response. No statement. No anything.

Now, students like Erick have to figure out what's next. I asked him what he plans on doing with his high school diploma from New Spiritual.

"Trash it, I guess. It doesn't really mean anything," he replied.

His mother summed up the situation this way, "He's 18, and you find an easier, softer way to be able to achieve a goal, and Baltimore County backing it up at the same time? I mean, it's like a no-brainer, in my opinion. I mean, we've always taught our kids that hard work pays off, and when you have something like this, this teaches kids the complete opposite."

One Baltimore County school board member did speak with us about the situation, saying, "That's really concerning, and it's a sad story. That tells me there is an industry developing around, in many cases, our school systems failing children, failing because they are not meeting the requirements for graduation."

* * *

This series of reports generated a huge response from the community.

Email to Project Baltimore: "I attended New Spiritual Christian foundation back in 2011. I've been reaching out to different people trying to get help because I put my money into that diploma."

Voice Message: "I'm calling because I am a concerned parent. My son also attended that New Spiritual Christian Academy."

Voice Message: "I am a former graduate, or supposedly graduate, from there, but it's not legit."

Voice Message: "Now, to actually see on the news and know that it was a problem. I'm at a loss and just want to know what happens from here on."

Voice Message: "No one should be charged to receive a high school diploma. It should be free."

Voice Message: "I really want to warn people about this program and how it's really interrupting. It interfered with my life and my livelihood, and even my health. It did cause me a lot of stress, not being able to get into any schools."

Others defended the school, saying it opened doors.

Email to Project Baltimore: "That new spiritual school u are talking about changed my wife's life completely."

Email to Project Baltimore: "I was one who took that route and I was able to further my education. I was able to attend be Morgan State University."

We produced a number of reports on New Spiritual over a period of a few days. A week or so after our story aired with Bridgeforth walking out, he called me. He said he was looking for a new building (one that met code and was zoned appropriately) to reopen his school. He also said he paid his debts to the state, and his school was now in good standing with the tax department.

Bridgeforth then asked if I would consider removing the stories from our website. I said no. But I did express interest in speaking with former New Spiritual students. He agreed.

This time, we met Bridgeforth on his terms. Not at Fox45, but at a church near his school, or row home. It was a bit awkward when we arrived. The church was in a run-down area of the city. He asked us to set up in the basement. It was very dark and late in the evening. His school had already been suspended. He was out of a job and desperate.

But I really wanted to interview his students. We needed them to offer insight into how a program like Bridgeforth's can operate for more than a decade. Who are his students, and what did the school do for them? We spoke with three women who all said they graduated from New Spiritual.

"We're not here to come and tear him down. We are with him," explained Cindy Williams.

"I will not allow ya'll to destroy it, to deceive it," Rachel Hanson added, "Mr. Kirk has had plenty of success, and I am one of them sitting in your face."

"When you get that piece of paper, I believe I can do the impossible," said Terrie White. "I can go anywhere with this high school diploma."

Williams, Hanson and White were certainly passionate.

"I said it's a witch hunt," White says. She dropped out of school in the tenth grade and had kids young. In 2015, she enrolled in New Spiritual. Three months later, she got her diploma and is now a nurse's assistant.

"We are here to discuss positive things. So, we're not going to allow anybody to come into our community and tear down what he has built up." Williams tried free GED classes. But dropped out. She paid New Spiritual, did the work, got a diploma and is now working.

"This paper really means something. It really does. I didn't know how much it meant until I was like, 'So you won't hire me because I don't have a high school diploma?' One thing out of all the skills that I can do. This one paper meant a lot." Hanson says she's a machinist; a job she needed a diploma to get.

All three agree—being able to say they have a high school diploma helped them get jobs.

But Dinkins at the Druid Heights Community Development Center worries that that "piece of paper" doesn't represent a quality education.

"They're not affiliated with a school," said Dinkins. "They're not affiliated with a college. They're not affiliated with the GED program itself."

In Maryland, if you create a church, you can also start a school, charge money and issue diplomas, and state law allows it.

"Education is so very important, and everyone should take it seriously. I would really plead with Maryland to maybe look into changing that," added Dinkins. "That's not fair to our citizens of Baltimore at all."

* * *

In response to our reporting on New Spiritual, the Maryland State legislature drafted a bill mandating that the State Department of Education, every year, would provide local municipalities with a list of non-public schools so safety, code and fire checks can be performed. The bill passed the Maryland House of Delegates 118 to 17. But it never made it out of the Education, Health and Environmental Affairs Senate Committee.

Committee members argued a new law wasn't necessary to keep students in church exempt schools safe. In return, the State Department of Education agreed to conduct regular site visits to ensure church exempt schools are following safety and fire codes.

But the educational aspect was never addressed. The private school community saw any changes in religious school autonomy as a slippery slope that could affect legitimate church organizations, of which Maryland has many.

As the legal aspect played out in Annapolis, we had largely exhausted all journalistic angles concerning church exempt schools, their autonomy, state safety checks and curriculum. Now, there was just one thing left to do—test the system.

Lawyers play a heavy role in the world of investigative journalism. What we do inevitably opens avenues for potential lawsuits. After an I-Team writes a script, it's often heavily scrutinized by a broadcast attorney to limit legal risk. Their job is to make sure news organizations don't get sued. Ergo, lawyers have the ability to kill stories. They often do. Or they neuter stories by removing so much content that the story isn't worth publishing.

In my career, I've worked with good and bad broadcast attorneys. Thankfully, the broadcast attorney we had during the New Spiritual series was a good one. I'll never forget the day I called him with our idea.

"Hello, Chris," said our attorney when he took my call. He had a very deep radio voice. Lots of bass.

"Hi Stephen," I replied. "How are you?"

"I'm well, Chris. How can I help you?"

My pitch was short. "Hey, so, you know the stories we've been doing on the church-exempt schools?"

"I do," he said.

"Yeah, about that," I paused. "We want to create our own church and start our own school."

I heard nothing. For a few seconds, nothing at all.

So, I continued. "We want to see how easy it really is to issue diplomas certified by the state of Maryland."

He released a long sigh . . . "Okayyyy . . . I've never heard that one before."

My pitch was made. It was that simple. Then, I just waited for a response.

"Let me look into the laws and get back to you," he stated.

At this point, I was feeling pretty good. Journalists can't misrepresent themselves in the pursuit of a report. So long as I didn't make money selling fake diplomas to unsuspecting members of the public, I figured I'd be fine to pursue my idea.

"I'll get back to you tomorrow," he said. "Does that work?"

I smiled. "Perfect."

A few weeks later, while the state was busy visiting all 500 or so church-exempt schools to make sure they were safe, Project Baltimore was busy creating its own church and school right under their noses. And we learned it's an easy two-step process.

Step one: we needed a church.

We grabbed our undercover cameras and drove to the Maryland Department of Assessments and Taxation.

"You want to do what?" the receptionist asked when our executive producer walked in. I did not go in. I couldn't take the chance of someone recognizing me.

"File the paperwork to start a church-exempt school," responded our EP.

"Oh, not a problem," she replied with a smile. "Do you want to expedite that or just drop it off?"

Twenty-nine minutes later, (Yes, 29 minutes later) the Church of Good News was created. We now had our very own church recognized by the state as a religious establishment with its own Tax ID number, for an expedited cost of $219.

Step two: apply to create a school.

We used a random building a few miles from our office as an address. The paperwork took about ten minutes to fill out. We then mailed it and waited. A few weeks later, Good News Academy was officially founded. I can't tell you how exciting it was when we saw Good News Academy listed by the Maryland State Department of Education as an active church-exempt school in Baltimore County. With little effort, Fox45 now had the ability to apply for state funding or charge for diplomas because Good News Academy was approved and certified by the Maryland State Department of Education.

"Completely unacceptable," replied Governor Larry Hogan. We sat down with the governor in his mansion for the final story we produced on this topic. Governor Hogan told Fox45, after our first report on church-exempt schools, he directed the Department of Education to launch a statewide compliance investigation while tightening registration requirements. That is how New Spiritual got shut down.

"The next morning," explained Hogan, "I had a staff meeting and I said this is absurd and ridiculous and we have to get to the bottom of it. The balance here is that there are small churches that have small schools that are legitimate. The ones you uncovered are blatantly committing fraud."

Hogan continued, "The Maryland State Department of Education needs to do a better job of investigating to make sure fraud is not taking place in selling diplomas from these phony operations. It's not something I think anyone in the Department of Education, or the Department of Assessments and Taxation, was aware of until you uncovered it. It's definitely fraud. It's a crime, and people need to be prosecuted."

After we told the governor we created our own church and school, both were removed from the state websites. We then disbanded both organizations.

CHAPTER 11

WHAT IS ALSO POSSIBLE

Education is one of those rare topics that is local, regional, and national. Public schools receive local, state, and federal tax dollars. And much of that money, as we have discussed, is tied to school data. There are billions of dollars up for grabs and tracking that money has become an arduous task.

I have had people tell me the problem with education is, at some point, too much money got involved. That sounds counter to everything we hear from politicians who claim, ad nauseam, that schools are underfunded. But there are people, many of whom work in education, who claim the opposite. They argue that as education spending increased by the billions, many people began to view public education not as a mechanism through which students are educated, but rather as a means to acquire wealth. Ergo, the reason to choose a career in public education may not be as altruistic as it once was.

The following was a five-part series Project Baltimore produced in 2019 about a city charter school that won a $1.5 million grant from the U.S. Department of Education and then shut down. This series, which we entitled *Fooling the Feds*, illustrates what is also possible by reinforcing

McDonalds' claim that, *"everything* is about data. And data means money." In this instance, we're talking about a lot of money—$500 million.

Pastor Dr. Cecil Gray was a hard man to find. Tall, thin, and always dressed like a priest, he never seemed to be in one place for too long. We went to his house, his church, and the two schools he ran in Baltimore City. It took us weeks, but we eventually found him. We tracked down Gray on behalf of taxpayers and parents like Justin Miller and Dayna White.

"Are you worried?" I didn't need to ask Miller and White that question. Their countenance said plenty.

"Very worried," replied Miller.

White nodded, "Well, of course."

Miller and White had two sons at Northwood Appold Community Academy, a charter elementary school in East Baltimore. The month after we interviewed them, NACA was set to shut down. City Schools' Board of Commissioners did not renew its charter. Even though the school received a $1.5 million federal grant just one year earlier.

"I feel like it's a slap in the face to us," Miller said, clearly upset. And for good reason. His children and 160 others were now scrambling to find a new school. And they didn't see it coming.

"First, we're looking for what kind of extracurricular activities they have for my son," explained White as she listed the traits she sought in their next school.

"Transportation," added Miller.

"Test scores?" I asked.

"Of course," Miller replied. "That's the main problem."

I followed up, "What's that process like?"

Again, they didn't have to answer. Their body language said enough.

"Hectic," stated White.

Miller affirmed, "Very frustrating."

A few months prior to our interview with the couple, Gray, the operator of NACA addressed the Baltimore City Board of School Commissioners—fighting to save his school.

"Underperforming? Not NACA," Gray testified, with a melodic cadence. "We have outperformed the city in every year of our existence. Ranks in the bottom five percent of Title I schools, false again."

His efforts failed. The board voted eight to one to shut down his school.

"I'm irate with the schools," said White, speaking of NACA.

Irate because this wasn't supposed to happen. Not even a year and a half earlier, NACA won a $1.5 million expansion grant from the U.S. Department of Education. Only 17 charter schools nationwide got this grant. The federal government must have been impressed. But the following year, City Schools shut it down. How can that happen? We obtained a copy of NACA's grant application from the federal government. We wanted to see what Gray told the feds to get your money.

The 60-page application described a school that has helped its students overcome poverty and violence. Apparently, NACA uses "Socratic seminars" and "equitable pedagogy" to consistently outperform its city and state peers.

It's right there on page 11—NACA's 2013 reading scores eight points higher than the state average. Sounds impressive—except it's not true. We pulled the data from the State Department of Education. NACA's reading scores were actually below the state average.

2013 English (grades 3-5)

	NACA	City	MD
Application	82	67	74
Actual	82	70	86
	(93/113)	(12,644/17,976)	(163,391 out of 189,070)

The graph below is similar. The application claims NACA's 2013 math scores were six points better than Maryland's average. But state data show they're actually eight points below.

2013 Math (grades 3-5)

	NACA	City	MD
Application	76	66	70
Actual	76	69	84
	(86/113)	(12,505/17,953)	(158,709/189,082)

What about suspensions? NACA reported to the federal government "seven suspensions over the past five years," much lower than state averages. But when we pulled City Schools' records, we counted 51 suspensions at NACA in the five years leading up to the grant.

Also, in his application, Dr. Gray says he communicates with families using the NACA Mobile App. So, we downloaded the App and found nothing. It was never set up.

And then there's this: in the application, NACA told the federal government it plans to have nearly 1,000 students enrolled in three schools by 2021 and the $1.5 million grant would help get them there. The problem is, NACA doesn't have three schools. It never did. The third was supposed to be built in West Baltimore. But it never became a reality. The application for a third school was never approved by the city.

"Where is this money going?" asked Miller. "If you got this money last year, y'all can't even keep the grass cut. The kids are playing in dirt in the back, in wood chips."

Miller was growing increasingly upset as he spoke. "These kids can't even go on a field trip. My son is ten years old, and they haven't even taken him to the aquarium, the zoo. Nothing, nothing, nothing. I'm really angry now. This is crazy."

Project Baltimore tried to get answers from NACA's founder, Dr. Gray. We emailed three times. With no reply, we started calling. We reached out to his attorney, his cell phone, and his church, Northwood United Methodist. We also contacted both of his schools, NACA and its high school, NACA II.

The receptionist at NACA told me, "He doesn't hold an office here, try NACA II."

The receptionist at NACA II told me, "He doesn't hold an office here."

Ten messages later, nothing. So, we started knocking. First, Gray's Baltimore County countryside home. Then, both schools and his church. We left business cards and more messages. Still nothing.

We wanted to know, did Gray misrepresent his school to get $1.5 million from taxpayers? So, we waited for him at his church for two days. When he finally arrived, he quickly left again. We tailed him to a parking lot where we finally got a chance to approach him.

Gray drove a black Genesis with chrome wheels and tinted glass. When he pulled into the parking lot, he quickly got out and walked into a nearby building. Seconds later, he reemerged and put some items in his trunk. As he got back into his car, I walked up. My cameraman was recording just a few steps behind me. Our producer was recording on the other side of the street, getting a wide view.

"Dr. Gray, Chris Papst with Fox45 news," I announced myself clearly. He opened the car door for a split second, then shut it.

"We've been trying to get a hold of you." I was now standing beside his car. We were separated by mere feet. "We wanted to ask you a few questions about the Department of Education grant you recently received."

Gray wasted no time. He put his car in reverse and started backing out into the street. I followed him to the sidewalk.

"Dr. Gray, can you answer just a few of our questions?" I hollered. "We've been trying to get a hold of you."

Without saying anything, he drove away.

* * *

The questions we had regarding the federal grant were not limited to where the money went. I was curious to learn how NACA got the money in the first place. And our investigation found the federal government may not have checked the facts before handing over your tax dollars, but we did.

"She says that she's okay, but she really don't know what's coming up." Parents like Michelle Robinson knew tough times were ahead.

"I'm worried about my baby adapting," she told me.

Just like White and Miller, Robinson was looking for a new school. And she was running out of time. When we spoke with her, she had just learned her daughter's school, NACA, was closing. She only had a few months to find a new school for her child.

Lakita Knott's situation was identical. "Where am I going to send my second grader, my soon-to-be second grader? There aren't any schools I want to send him to."

"We're looking into private school because this was my last choice for a city public school," added another parent.

North Avenue's review of NACA's charter, which precipitated the board's vote, was harsh. It labeled the school as "not effective" in test scores and "governance." And it says going back to 2015, "The school has a pattern of Title I noncompliance which places the entire district's Title I award at risk."

Title I funding is federal funding to help schools in high-poverty areas. Why is this important? Remember, just about a year before the school board vote, NACA received that $1.5 million grant from the U.S. Department of Education. That means, while NACA was not complying with the federal government, according to City Schools, the federal government was awarding the school more than a million dollars.

"I don't find it terribly surprising," said Max Eden, with the Manhattan Institute, a center-right think tank.

City Schools told Fox45 the feds don't contact them with questions before a grant is issued. Max Eden specializes in federal education policy.

"I think Department of Education bureaucrats are generally known as kind of compliance box checkers, and thinking to fact check what they're being presented in a grant application is something that the ones I know—I can see not really occurring to them," he said.

Had the federal government checked some facts before issuing the grant, here's what else they may have learned about NACA.

- Documents obtained by Fox45 showed that in 2017, the year the grant was issued, NACA was reprimanded at least three times by North Avenue for "non-compliance" and "unprofessional conduct."
- City Schools has publicly stated during board meetings that NACA has violated FERPA, the federal Family Education Rights and Privacy Act, has a history of non-compliance with contractual obligations and is "Not effective" in managing grants.
- In 2016 and 17, NACA's high school, had zero students proficient in Algebra I.

But that's still not all, had the feds simply Googled NACA, they likely would have seen the 2017 Fox45 investigation into NACA II. The grade-changing reports we produced for the high school aired <u>one month</u> before the grant was issued. NACA II was the school where we had that test issued to seniors.

Remember this quote from Yellow Flowers, who was a teacher at NACA II?

"What I did was I put the grades in. If someone changed the grades, that was on them."

We had report cards and interviewed teachers who said students who failed required courses still graduated.

"Do you really think the Department of Education is looking at these applications?" I asked Eden.

"Not closely enough to double check," he replied. "I think it's all part and parcel of the way that education governance works with the federal government."

The U.S. Department of Education declined an interview with Fox45, but they explained in a statement that "all grant applications are reviewed to verify whether the applicant is eligible to receive a grant. Department staff review each application to verify the accuracy of the information. The [ED] also conducts an Entity Risk Review to verify the financial viability of the applicant and its satisfactory performance under other Federal programs." This was written by Jim Bradshaw from the U.S. Department of Education press office.

Keep in mind, annually, the U.S. Department of Education awards nearly $500 million of taxpayers' dollars in grants. The most deserving charter schools in America are supposed to get the money.

"I can't imagine this is the only time it's happened," added Eden. "Is this happening a handful of times? Ten percent of the time? Thirty percent of the time? Has anybody ever checked into this?"

We mentioned the federal government doesn't contact City Schools before issuing grants. The Maryland State Department of Education told us the feds don't contact the state either. Maybe if they had, the ED would have known about the problems at NACA before handing over $1.5 million.

* * *

The grant that NACA received was so rare that, at the time, only one other charter school in Maryland had ever won it. As I started looking into it, I learned that what happened with both schools after they received the grant was very different. But what happened before was exactly the same.

"The moment, though, you found out you got the grant, that had to be a really exciting moment," I asked Laura Doherty, from the Baltimore Curriculum Project.

She laughed, "That was really exciting. It was a real validation of our plan. Not only do we think we're doing the right thing, but the Department of Education thinks we're doing the right thing as well."

Doherty remembers that day in 2015 very well. The day her charter school became the first in Maryland to win a prestigious expansion grant from the U.S. Department of Education. That year, just twelve schools nationwide won this particular grant, totaling $85 million. Doherty's school got nearly $300,000 of that ($282,720).

"We were thrilled," she told me.

Doherty runs the Baltimore Curriculum Project, the largest charter school operator in Baltimore City. They have five schools. The grant went to Govans Elementary in North Baltimore.

"Govans is a really great school. It's a somewhat hidden gem," explained Doherty.

Doherty tells Project Baltimore some of the grant was used for marketing—pamphlets, brochures, their sign out front, etc. But most went for an academic coach for the school's teachers. It appears to have worked. Govans' test scores have significantly increased. At the time we produced this report, English proficiency had nearly tripled. Math scores were also up.

Maryland State Test Scores

	ELA	Math
2016	7	13
2017	14	14
2018	20.5	18.5

Source: Maryland State Department of Education

"We're really pleased," said Doherty, speaking of the school's improved academics.

For two years, Govans remained the only school in Maryland to receive this grant. But in 2017, they were joined by Northwood Appold Community Academy, which got $1.5 million in taxpayer dollars.

To quickly recap (because it's worth reiterating), Project Baltimore's investigation raised some serious questions about how and why NACA got this grant. We looked at the school's grant application and found the numbers didn't add up. For example, NACA told the federal government its 2013 reading scores were eight points higher than the state average. But according to the State Department of Education, they were actually lower.

Plus, despite winning that $1.5 million grant, the Baltimore City School Board voted, in January, to close NACA, saying it had a "pattern" of not complying with federal education law and was deemed "not effective" in managing grants.

When we tried to ask NACA's founder, Dr. Cecil Gray, about all of this, he refused to speak with us. But North Avenue told Project Baltimore that before issuing grants, the U.S. Department of Education does not contact local school systems to ask questions.

The ED declined an on-camera interview but is taking action to correct the issues Project Baltimore has exposed. One week after we broke this story, we received this statement from the ED's press secretary:

> "The department is committed to being a good steward of taxpayer dollars and holding all grantees accountable. Any instance of fraud, waste, and abuse will be investigated. All grant applications go through a rigorous peer review process. And, while the process is a long-established one across the federal government, the Department is working internally to improve how grant applications are reviewed and scored."—Elizabeth Hill

That brings us back to Govans, where I asked Doherty this question, "Nobody ever contacted you? You just found out one day that you got the grant?"

"I don't think they ever contacted us to interview us," she replied. "I know they didn't come to the school. I don't think there was any contact once you submitted the grant until getting notified that you got it."

No visits. No phone calls. No emails. No anything.

"We need to create schools that families really want to bring their kids to," explained Doherty. "And where all the kids are successful. And they are fun, lively places for people to be. That's our goal."

Since winning the grant from the U.S. Department of Education, Doherty told Project Baltimore the feds do conduct audits and quarterly phone calls. So, after the grant is issued, Doherty says the ED is in contact with the school. But not before.

For the record, it's worth pointing out that the Maryland State Department of Education also gives out grants. And Doherty told me that when the state issues grants to schools, they do visit the school and interview the people at the school before making any final decisions on who gets the money.

* * *

The idea of charter schools has taken off in America. They're meant to foster new ideas in education and receive tax dollars based on student enrollment. But they have more freedom to spend that money than traditional schools. But as our investigation into NACA's grant expanded, we began asking if the academic and monetary freedom afforded to charter schools comes with enough accountability.

No one talks about 990s. Few people even know what they are. But we spent months going line by line through years of 990s filed by Dr. Cecil Gray, who, we learned, not only runs a church and two charter schools in Baltimore, but also operated a foundation.

What we found inside those 990s, in part, is why we spent weeks trying to track down Dr. Gray and approached him in that parking lot. It was vital that we tried to ask him the questions that arose from our research.

To briefly explain, 990s are financial statements that non-profits file with the IRS every year. The question is, who's checking them?

"A school will disclose things about its finances. But if there is no government agency with the power and resources to actually examine the disclosures, they're not very meaningful." Susan DeJarnatt is a law professor at Temple University. For 20 years, she's written extensively about oversight and accountability of charter schools. One of her topics is 990s.

"Somebody's got to look at this stuff to make sure that the schools are doing what they need to be doing in terms of finances," said DeJarnatt.

Her city, Philadelphia, has around 80 charter schools. DeJarnatt says that at one point, 19 were under federal investigation. She believes, if local school boards and other authorities looked for red flags in charter school 990s, it could reduce the number of investigations, which are time-consuming and expensive.

Stated DeJarnatt, "I certainly would never say all of them were criminal. That's absolutely not true. But it's troubling because the possibility for misuse seems high."

Here's the story Dr. Gray's 990s, at the time, told us that could be considered red flags. As we mentioned, Gray had a foundation, two schools, and a church. His foundation was based in his home. His school was based at his church. He was the head of all four. We can't see what money his church gets. Churches don't have to file 990s. But his school and foundation did. Here's what we found:

- Foundations generally rely on donations. But from 2008 to 2017, Gray moved nearly $1.4 million from his schools to his foundation—nearly all its funding—with a stated mission to "support development of educational programs and institutions."

- However, almost all of the foundation's money, about 90 percent, was paid out in salaries. Gray paid himself $126,500 a year.

- And he paid his employees well. In 2017, the year he won that million-dollar federal grant, Gray's foundation paid its secretary nearly $57,000 ($56,934) for one hour of work a week. That comes to $1,100 an hour.

- In 2014, 2015, and 2016, Gray paid a co-secretary an average of $37,021 for five hours of work a week—$142 an hour.

We can't see that any money, other than salaries, in 2017 was actually spent on the foundation's stated mission, "educational programs" or "institutions."

"Does that surprise you?" I asked DeJarnatt.

"Sadly, no, it doesn't surprise me," she replied.

City Schools declined an interview with Project Baltimore to discuss its charter review process, but told us 990s are not part of it. The U.S. Department of Education told us they also don't look at 990s. DeJarnatt says if someone, anyone, would look at 990s, maybe a school on the verge of shutting down wouldn't receive a $1.5 million federal grant.

"If you look up almost any newspaper article circa 1999 to 2005, that article will describe charter schools as an innovation that allows greater freedom in exchange for greater accountability, but what is that greater accountability?" concluded DeJarnatt.

* * *

What we have already learned from this investigation is that the U.S. Department of Education doesn't appear to do its homework before awarding millions of your tax dollars in charter school grants. But now, get this. We also discovered that NACA was getting money from the federal government even as its owner was in trouble with the federal government.

This is hard to believe. But a simple public records search could have told the U.S. Department of Education all it needed to know as it was awarding more than $1.5 million to a school that was shut down soon after. Apparently, they didn't do it.

When we produced this report, we spoke with a former teacher at NACA.

"What did you think when you saw those stories?" I asked him.

"Finally." We agreed to conceal this man's identity to protect his job. But he agreed we could use his pronouns. NACA had a number of male teachers.

"When I saw your second story, I then realized, well, I now definitely need to speak up," he said. "When I saw your report, it all made sense."

NACA gets the same funding as any other charter in the city. But this teacher says the school always seemed to have money problems. Project Baltimore often hears about a lack of basic resources in City Schools. But at NACA, this teacher says it was on another level.

"We questioned why we were being given limited resources." His frustration was palpable. "Why weren't we able to make copies? Why didn't we have a curriculum? Why weren't there any textbooks? I didn't have a bulletin board in my classroom, a dry erase board, a Promethean, nothing. We taught on paper and pencil."

He paused to gather his thoughts and his breath. "Paper was a huge issue. We didn't understand why we were being limited to paper. I mean, we were teachers that were teaching as if we were teaching in a third world country, essentially like we had no resources, just us and the students."

Throwing his hands up in the air, he stated, "We started to question where the money was going."

With all that in mind, when Project Baltimore told this teacher about our latest discovery in our investigation of NACA, he wasn't surprised.

"I saw it, I saw it, I know it. I mean, we all saw it," he responded.

What we found is that the federal government doesn't appear to check with the federal government before issuing grants. In September of 2018, the IRS placed a $44,093 tax lien on Northwood Appold Methodist Church.

Why is this important? Well, Gray is the pastor of that church. And NACA sits on the church's property. So, at the exact time the federal government awarded Gray's school a $1.5 million grant, Gray hadn't paid his church's federal taxes for three years.

The U.S. Department of Education declined all requests for interviews, but told us in a statement, by Elizabeth Hill, as a result of this investigation, that the department is "working internally to improve how grant applications are reviewed and scored."

Throughout this entire investigation that spanned months, Dr. Gray never returned any of our calls or emails. And he never attempted to contact me after we tried to speak with him in that parking lot.

"It's almost confusing because you want to speak out. You want to say something about it because we see it every day," the NACA teacher explained. For teachers, speaking out can be a risk. "They can do things that make your life hard as a teacher."

But this educator says he came forward before more money, federal or local, is awarded to his former school.

"He hurt a lot of the kids that were coming out of that school," said the teacher, with clear remorse. "It was only a matter of time before people would start catching onto him."

The U.S. Department of Education told us, when we had first reported on NACA's grant application, they had paid $500,000 of the $1.5 million grant to the school. They also said the grant could be revoked and Dr. Gray could be asked to pay back the money he has already received.

After the fifth story in this series aired, the ED went silent on us. We tried for the next two years to get updates on Gray, NACA and the grant. The ED refused to answer any more questions.

In January 2020, Dr. Gray filed a $200,000,000 lawsuit against Fox45 News and me, claiming the media coverage ruined him financially and led to his schools being shut down. In October of 2021, the case went to a Baltimore City jury. I testified under oath over a two-day period regarding our reportage.

The jury entered a defense verdict, and Gray received nothing.

Viewer Voicemail: FOX45/Project Baltimore Tipline:

*"My name is ****** and my son ******* goes to BALTIMORE INTERNATIONAL ACADEMY. This is one of the schools that I know that just pass children on to the next grade ,even if they have a very low grade. Well, for the last two years, I've repeatedly asked can they hold him back because I KNOW HE NEEDS MORE TIME. Their reason for not holding him back is because he will eventually catch up (that's a lie, total lie). I know my child, and he's not getting concepts of a lot of his work. He is below grade average with a IEP. And that's not even working for him. This year he supposed to be in the fifth-grade classes, but they have him taking six-grade classes. My son is drowning even more because if he can't get the concept of the fifth-grade work why would they give him six-grade classes."*

CHAPTER 12

LEARNED HELPLESSNESS

Let's recap. In August 2017, Fox45 News aired its first report on alleged grade changing in Baltimore City Schools. In the following months, we produced dozens of reports on the topic and filed public records requests for documents related to internal grade-changing investigations within the district. In December of 2017, Fox45 sued Baltimore City Public Schools after our public records requests were denied, and the district gave us nothing.

Over the next fifteen months, North Avenue began to slowly release documents, many of which were fully redacted. Simultaneously, hundreds of employees and parents were telling us that students were being pushed through the school system without getting the education they needed.

In February of 2019, a Circuit Court Judge ruled in Fox45's favor, saying City Schools "willfully and knowingly" violated the law by not turning over the documents.

During the trial, North Avenue disclosed eleven grade-changing investigations pursuant to our request. But four months after the judge's ruling, in mid-2019, City Schools released 22 internal grade-changing investigations. Within one of the internal investigations, North Avenue's own investigator called the "rounding up" of failing grades to passing an "unwritten practice" and urged the school system to end the practice.

That brings us to the fall of 2020, nearly two years after we went to court, and North Avenue finally began to release the remainder of what the judge ordered. We received 8,249 emails sent by school employees concerning grade changing. We read all of them. Ever. Single. Email. We then separated them into groups and began to plan out a series of stories.

Before we get into the emails, let's get this part out of the way. North Avenue denied all interview requests. The front office refused to discuss the issue with us despite being forced by the judge to reimburse about $200,000 of our legal fees, which were all taxpayer dollars. Instead, we received this statement that read, in part:

> "As we have said consistently since the allegations were made, we take the integrity of grades extremely seriously. If grades do not accurately reflect what students have achieved, teachers cannot provide the instruction and support each student needs to succeed. That goes against our commitment to every student and family we serve. The documents obtained by Fox45, dating to 2017, reflect concerns that we did not ignore. Much has changed since that period."

The statement went on to explain how, in May of 2019, City Schools adopted a new grade-changing policy, which included additional training for grade reporters, and it required principals to notify teachers in writing before student grades are adjusted.

We produced a series of reports concerning the content of the 8,249 emails we received. What we found was truly stunning.

* * *

We often hear there's an unwritten rule in Baltimore City Schools where failing grades of 58 and 59 are rounded up to a passing grade of 60. Following a two-and-a-half-year court battle with North Avenue, we now had emails that showed it's not just 58 and 59 that get rounded up.

Inside the Baltimore City Public Schools headquarters, known as North Avenue, the education of about 75,000 city students is overseen by high-level personnel and administrators, including this one, whose identity we agreed to conceal.

"We're not helping students. We're not helping families. We're not helping to build the city." What's not helping, according to this administrator, is grade changing.

"What we see is when we graduate students, they become unemployable because they don't have those basic skills in order to maintain jobs," the educator explained.

We specifically asked the administrator about the 8,249 emails we received from the lawsuit. We started with Email 3898.

In this email, sent in February of 2018 at Patterson High School, a person with the title of master scheduler sent an email to school administrators saying, "Attached is a spreadsheet of the students that received a final grade of 58 and 59. Infinite Campus does not automatically round these grades to a 60 D-. In order to do so, please complete and sign the grade change form."

"If you're an administrator and you get that email, what is that email telling you to do?" I asked.

This was the answer: "That email was instructing me to complete the form to change the grade. This is common. I'm kind of shocked that it's in an email because typically things of this nature aren't put in writing. But this is something that is often discussed in team-level meetings and staff meetings in schools."

(Email 6143) In this email, a teacher who appears to be frustrated writes, "I am requesting that grades, being submitted by me, not be altered/changed."

(Email 6210) Here, a teacher is asked to change a grade "based on school policy." The teacher replies, "If this is the school policy, then I guess the grade should be changed . . . although I don't think she deserves it."

The administrator pointed out, "There is no such policy in the books."

(Email 7220) Then, there's an email where a principal writes, "I would like to inquire about how you would like us to proceed with grades from a 56-59 from the previous school year being bumped up to a 60."

"Have you seen failing grades as low as 56 get rounded up to a passing 60?" I asked.

"I've seen grades as low as a 49 get rounded up to a 60," the administrator responded.

That was shocking to hear. "A 49?!"

"Yes. It's indefensible," was the reply.

I followed up, "I mean, no extra work from the teacher, no extra assignments filled out by the student. Just rounding up from a 49 to a 60?"

"Yes."

This administrator says the pressure to round up grades starts with the Maryland State Department of Education, where districts are expected to increase graduation rates. That pressure is felt by superintendents and filters down to principals and teachers. This North Avenue employee says the answer is more rigorous instruction and more help for students who need it. But the administrator told Fox45, it's easier to just change a grade to promote students.

"I see that as being part of the culture in a number of Baltimore City Schools," stated the educator. "It gives the student a false sense of hope. From what I know of Baltimore City Schools being a part of it for a number of years, I feel as a parent who is aware of what's going on, I feel I [would] be totally negligent to allow my children to attend Baltimore City Public Schools."

* * *

As we work our way through these emails, keep in mind that Baltimore City Schools didn't want the public to see any of them. And, according to Judge Hong, the District was willing to break the law in order to do so.

It was January 26, 2019, when a teacher at Calverton Elementary/ Middle in West Baltimore wrote this email to her principal.

Teacher email: "I would like very much to never be asked to change any grades ever again."

That principal was Martia Cooper. If that name and that school sound familiar—they should.

Project Baltimore first broke the Calverton story in September of 2017. We spoke to a teacher who received a text message from Principal Cooper saying, "If you find any grade averages below 60, pkesss (sic) have REDACTED NAME correct." We also obtained two versions of report cards for thirteen students. In the first version, the students were failing. In the second, all thirteen had their grades changed to passing.

When we went to the school to try to speak with Cooper, she called the cops on us.

After our stories aired, City Schools, under then-Chief Academic Officer Sean Conley, launched an internal investigation, which confirmed improper grade changing was happening at Calverton. Yet, Principal Cooper kept her job.

All of this brings us back to that January 26, 2019 email a teacher sent to Principal Cooper about being asked to change grades. This email was sent thirteen months after North Avenue's own investigation confirmed improper grade changing was happening at Calverton. And apparently, according to this email, teachers were still being asked to change grades.

The teacher wrote in her email, "I have been asked by Ms. Brown to change the grades of two of my students. They are the two lowest students in my room. I feel it is unethical to bump them to the next level."

Principal Cooper replied in the email thread, "It is not our practice to ask teachers to change grades, and I have not known Ms. Brown to do so."

"This is not the first time I have been asked to do this," the teacher responded, "I was also asked in quarter one to do something similar."

In the final email, Ms. Brown denies asking the teacher to change grades. And we don't know if they were changed. The email chain ends there.

North Avenue declined an interview, reiterating in a statement that in May of 2019, City Schools adopted a new grade-changing policy that included a mandate that principals contact teachers before changing a grade and then notify the teacher in writing if the grade is changed.

The statement said, "The email exchange from Calverton in January 2019 is a clear example of why additional guidance was required.

Additionally, the email exchange is a discussion regarding the rationale for a grade from a teacher and is not grade changing. School leaders, at times, will discuss grades of students for a variety of reasons—being fair to students across the board being one of the main reasons."

We showed the January 2019 email thread to the same North Avenue administrator from earlier in this chapter.

"I'm not going to say that what we do in Baltimore City Schools is easy. But when we try to pass the buck, which is, as we pass students, it's kicking the can down the road," said the administrator.

This high-level employee sees it differently, saying over the years, a culture of grade changing has taken root in Baltimore City as a way to push failing students through the system. And over time, those years have become decades.

The administrator added, "In order to help build the city, this is something we have to tackle, the issue. And the issue is not just the kids that are not meeting with success now, but I dare say we have generations in Baltimore City that have not met with academic success."

* * *

"This is a damning letter. This makes my hands shake right here." For eleven years, Aaron Thompson was a teacher in Baltimore City Public Schools. He left in 2018. "This is exactly what I had to put up with."

His quivering hands struggled to stabilize the email, which I had printed out. "This letter seems to be making you angry," I said.

"Oh yeah. It's frustration," he shouted, violently jolting the paper. "When something's out of your control, that's what anger is."

Thompson was responding to one of the more than 8,000 emails City Schools only released after we sued to get them.

The email clearly triggered him. He ignited with indignance. "It's so hard to do the right thing when someone above you is telling you to do the wrong thing."

In the email, from February of 2017, an administrator at Northwestern High School asked a teacher to "consider a grade change" for a student who failed two classes with a 58 and 59.

The teacher responds, "I will NOT endorse a grade change."

The administrator replies, "We do not issue a grade of **59 for any student.** Therefore, I am suggesting that you review the issues again." The end of that first sentence was bolded and highlighted in the original email.

The teacher wrote back, "I gave him a makeup packet, and he never turned it in. He only attended my class 21 days (maybe) out of the 90 days. I literally used to run after him to give him work and tried to get him to come to class. I have zero work from him."

We don't know if the grade was changed. The email chain ends there.

Thompson said, "This administrator now knows this teacher won't play ball, and that's going to [have an] effect. And that just brings the whole culture of the school down."

Project Baltimore found other emails where teachers push back after being asked to change grades to promote students. In this email, from 2016, a teacher wrote:

(Email 3742) "The students have not completed all the requirements for graduation. Some of them have failed other classes, and teachers are being forced to change their grades. It seems the administration is more concerned about meeting quotas than with providing our students with a quality education and good values."

Thompson says this email could have been written by him about one of his own students. He proceeded to tell me he personally watched a student who could not read receive a high school diploma.

"He couldn't read that," Thompson declared. "A high school diploma from Baltimore City is a slap in the face to those kids who really do buckle down."

Thompson had a lot of passion. And he didn't care to hide it. Like most teachers, he sought the profession to help children succeed, especially children from underprivileged backgrounds. That is why he initially chose to work in Baltimore City. He said he left the district after realizing his goals appeared to differ from his employer's.

"You obviously send a child out into the world that doesn't know what they're supposed to know. However, everybody's happy. The child's happy. He's graduating. Mom's happy. He's graduating. The administrator's happy. The graduation rate went up," concluded Thompson.

* * *

Of the 8,249 emails we received from City Schools, one was so egregious, we could not find any public official, at the time, who was willing to address it on camera.

We reached out to Governor Larry Hogan, City Schools CEO Dr. Sonja Santelises, State Superintendent Dr. Karen Salmon, Baltimore

Mayor Jack Young, City Council President Brandon Scott, the Baltimore City Teachers Union and the Principals' Union. We even contacted the person who wrote the email. None of them agreed to an interview to discuss it.

But Aaron Thompson was more than willing to offer his thoughts, "I'd be banging on some doors. I'd be looking forward to the next staff meeting if I got this!" Thompson had never calmed down. He was still fired up.

Fellow former teacher Marvin Lee was also willing to discuss the email. Though his delivery was more mellow. "The teachers are held responsible for the kids, not the kids."

The email was written in 2016 by an assistant principal to his teachers at Green Street Academy. It starts with the assistant principal informing teachers that a "significant number of students had failing grades." He says he would never tell teachers to change a student's grade, but to "consider the long-term impact on their life trajectory." He then writes, "Unfortunately, we work in an environment where our students suffer from learned helplessness. They have been socially promoted from the time they were in kindergarten until they reached eighth grade. When they hit high school, we hold them to a standard that requires them to pass in order to earn a credit."

Thompson went off after reading those words.

"You said the problem!" yelled Thompson. "You said what the problem was. We've promoted them up until now, and now we're going to hold them accountable, but you have to understand they have learned helplessness, so you might want to change the grade. Make up your mind! Make up your mind. In fact, which way do you want to go here? They don't know how to succeed, so go ahead and let them succeed. Or are you going to hold them accountable? But you know, you might want to rethink that because it has a long-term impact on their life trajectory. You think social promotion doesn't have a long-term impact on their life trajectory?"

Social promotion is the practice of passing students to the next grade, no matter their skill level, to help their self-esteem. Remember, City Schools' regulations state a student can only fail a total of one grade prior to high school. The Green Street Academy's assistant principal appears to be saying because of that regulation, students "suffer from learned helplessness."

This email highlights a problem we hear often: that social promotion leads to some students being pushed through the system without getting the education they need. And your public officials, presiding over this educational approach, don't want to talk about it.

"The link has to be us getting better at what our accountability is as school administrators, superintendents, instead of just everybody just getting paid," opined Lee. "This has to be about, what are we actually going to teach our children?"

* * *

These emails offered insight into what was really happening inside Baltimore City Schools. And it convinced some to call for a deeper investigation.

"That's criminal," declared Clarence Mitchell IV. Mitchell, better known as C4, co-hosts the *C4 and Bryan Nehman* show, a popular morning drive radio talk show on WBAL Radio in Baltimore.

"It's horrible. But it's true," added his co-host, Bryan Nehman.

Mitchell replied with clear frustration, "8,249 emails were finally captured by Project Baltimore, and what they've uncovered is horrific!"

As previously mentioned, in the thousands of emails Project Baltimore received from this lawsuit, we found cases of failing grades rounded up to passing, students being promoted without showing up to class, and teachers feeling pressured to change grades. All of it raised concerns that students are being pushed through the system and not getting the education they need.

"If you want to know what is really, generationally, what is a problem in this city, it's the public education system doing things like this," stated Mitchell.

Nehman agreed, "It's pretty clear it's still continuing, and that is why I completely agree with you, either an outside source or the state needs to come in and take a closer look at what is going on."

Mitchell called for one specific person. "The inspector general, specifically, Richard Henry. This is why this office was set up, Bryan."

Richard Henry is Maryland's first Inspector General for Education (OIGE). He was appointed in 2020 by Governor Larry Hogan, when the office was established. He's assigned to investigate fraud, waste and abuse in public education statewide. Concerning his office opening an investigation into grade changing in City Schools, he told Project Baltimore, "We are aware of the matter and currently looking into the allegations."

Fox45 News also reached out to state lawmakers and Baltimore City Council members to see if they support an IG investigation. Councilman Isaac Schleifer and Delegate Frank Conaway said they would support it.

Councilman Bill Henry told us in a statement: "All agencies and departments that receive tax dollars from Baltimore City residents should be regularly & intentionally scrutinized and audited."

"Seventy percent of the money from Baltimore City's school system is coming from state tax dollars," explained Mitchell to his audience. "We spend so much money on taxes, that is why we should demand accountability from these school systems."

Baltimore City Schools also declined a request to be on the *C4 and Bryan Nehman* show to discuss the emails. Instead, the hosts read their audience the City Schools statement concerning the district adopting a new grade-changing policy in May of 2019.

"What in the hell was going on before May of 2019? What was going on?" asked Mitchell.

You could almost hear Nehman shaking his head, "Who knows?"

Mitchell's voice grew with intensity the more he discussed our findings. The former State Delegate and State Senator is from Baltimore City. He has seen the consequences of a failing public education system. "If you have to change your policy because of what was found through investigative reporting, and conditions of anonymity for witnesses who saw things, what were you doing? That's rhetorical."

Mitchell left his listeners with this thought.

"Educational malpractice. Educational criminality. Whatever you want to call it. Everybody, stay tuned. Because we really have to do better by the kids."

* * *

The emails we received from the lawsuit didn't just show some students had their grades changed; we also found the issues went far beyond grade changing. It appears some students were given grades without doing any work.

Marvin Lee has been a master barber in Baltimore for nearly 40 years. Soft spoken and thoughtfully articulate, barbering is a life he loves and loves to share, which is why in 2003, he began teaching barbering for Baltimore City Public Schools.

"This class here was my first class, which was my senior class," Lee explained, as he displayed an old class photo.

By his second year of teaching, Lee says he noticed something wasn't right. He says students who received a failing grade somehow ended up passing his class. Lee says he believes someone was just giving students grades to pass them along.

"It's ridiculous. It's sad," Lee told me.

Lee spent five years in City Schools. He left in 2008.

"I actually walked away from something that I had passion for based off of the culture." He was not proud of his decision to leave City Schools. But he couldn't operate with a good conscience in that culture.

And that culture, which he says was a problem back then, appears to be the same today. We showed Lee some of the emails we received from the lawsuit.

"I'm not shocked by this email," he said. "I was told the exact same."

The first email we showed him, from 2016, was from an Assistant Principal at Edmondson-Westside High School. It explained that "there are missing grades" for students who "entered the class late." It appears the solution was not to teach the students the material they missed. Rather, the administrator told teachers to give "the student the same grade (in the quarter they missed) he/she earned in the quarter that you taught [them]."

Lee says, based on his experience, that the email could have been written fifteen years earlier when he was a teacher.

"This is not surprising at all, this is normal," Lee said. "They tell you what to put down."

Another email chain we showed him from 2016 starts with an assistant principal at Dunbar High School writing, "Any student who did not come and take a midterm exam should get a grade of 40."

A school coach quickly responds, "Tell me, how does this make sense!!!!!! 40 even for a no show????"

Another teacher replies, "If my kids didn't take the exam, they get a zero," saying that school leaders are "trying to make the data look better."

And another teacher responds, writing, "That is absolutely irresponsible and violates the integrity of the institution."

Lee added, "Basically, Chris, I'm telling you all of this is just too familiar." Conjuring these stored memories was not pleasant for him. "Most of the time I was there, I was pretty much babysitting. That's what they made us. I wasn't able to really teach my course."

He continued, "It's about the change. We're in a time now where we're doing everything against what's right."

Over the years, Lee had clearly reflected back and assembled his thoughts on what he observed working for Baltimore City Schools.

"We got smart and bright kids," he said. "I mean, these kids aren't failing because they can't do it. They're failing because they know they can—that's the difference."

* * *

Three years after we first filed that initial public records request, we finally had everything we requested. And it confirmed what parents, teachers and students had been telling us, that many students were being pushed through the school system—often graduating—without the basic skills to succeed in life. The public school system, set up to help students, has failed many of them for generations. And instead of being transparent, the leaders of that system were willing to go to court and spend a lot of money to cover up the proof.

In the end, there are real-life consequences for the young people involved. Baltimore continues to be one of the poorest and most violent cities in America. Yet, the adults who oversee the school system continue to see their funding increase from $1.3 billion in 2017 to $1.7 billion in 2024. And this funding increase has occurred as enrollment has plummeted from 82,354 in 2017 to 75,811 in 2024. In other words, Baltimore City Schools continues to get more money to educate fewer students.

Even though we now had everything pursuant to our public records request, our investigation was still not over. As we reported above, our reporting caught the attention of Rick Henry, the Maryland Inspector General for Education. Our work inspired him to launch his own investigation into the school system. We would have to wait until mid-2022 for his report. But it would be worth it. Because he has something we in the media don't have—subpoena power.

CHAPTER 13

"FAILURE FACTORY"

When it comes to explosive reports exposing the failures of Baltimore City Public Schools, what happened at Augusta Fells Savage may be the most egregious.

Most parents who contact the media seeking help are desperate. It's often a last resort. No one wants to go on camera to publicly air their struggles. But when it comes to their children, agony often results in action.

That was certainly true of Tiffany France. When Fance called Fox45's newsroom, she was completely lost. And we were, too. France was so flustered, her message made no sense. When I called her back, she was an emotional mess. After our conversation, I still didn't know what her story was. But she was so upset, I figured we should interview her. And I was so glad we did.

This was the headline when France's story aired: *City student passes 3 classes in four years, ranks near top half of class with 0.13 GPA*

That headline would eventually go viral and become the most viewed story in the history of Fox45's website. Millions of people, from around the world, clicked on that headline, and for good reason. France's story would snowball to eventually consume the entire state.

"He's stressed, and I am too. I told him I'm probably going to start crying. I don't know what to do for him," cried France during our initial interview. She was inconsolable. France lived in South Baltimore. A fashion expert by trade, she wore long nails and big hair with confidence. But for our interview, she was out of her element.

"I'm just trying to fight. He's like, 'Mom, what was all this for? What did I do this for?' Don't he get a chance? Do he get a chance?" We interviewed France in February of 2021. That coming June, she thought her son would receive his high school diploma. But after four years of high school, she had just learned, her 17-year-old had to start over. He was moved back to ninth grade.

"Why would he do three more years in school? He didn't fail, the school failed him." She struggled to hold back the tears as her voice cracked under the pressure. "The school failed at their job. They failed. They failed, that's the problem here. They failed. They failed. He didn't deserve that."

France's son attended the Augusta Fells Savage Institute of Visual Arts in West Baltimore. His transcripts showed that in four years, he passed just three classes, earning 2.5 credits, placing him in ninth grade. But France says she didn't know that until February of what she thought was his senior year.

France, a single mom, had three children and worked three jobs. She thought her oldest son was doing well because even though he failed most of his classes, he was being promoted through the grades. His transcripts showed he failed Spanish I and Algebra I, but was promoted to Spanish II and Algebra II. He also failed English II, but was passed on to English III.

"I'm just assuming that if you are passing, that you have the proper things to go to the next grade and the right grades, you have the right credits," she explained.

As we dug deeper into her son's records, we could see that in his first three years at Augusta Fells, he failed 22 classes and was late or absent 272 days. But in those three years, only one teacher requested a parent conference, which France says never happened. No one from the school told this mother her son was failing and not going to class.

France's son, in his four years at Augusta Fells, earned a GPA of 0.13. He only passed three classes. But his transcripts showed something incredible—his class rank was 62 out of 120. At first, we thought it had to be a typo. It wasn't. That class rank meant that nearly half his classmates, 58 of them, had a 0.13 grade point average or lower. This story was not about one student. It was about dozens of students, which turned into hundreds of students, and then thousands.

"That school community failed this student," stated a City Schools administrator who works inside North Avenue. This long-time employee asked not to be identified. You know, for fear of retaliation. But for this story, we felt we needed the context of someone from the inside.

The administrator explained that City Schools failed because it has protocols and interventions set up to help students who are falling behind or have low attendance. In France's son's case, those interventions were not utilized.

"I get angry," stated the administrator. "There's nothing but frustration. We see on the news the crime that occurs, the murders, the shootings. We know that there are high levels of poverty in Baltimore. And at this juncture, things like this are adding to that. It is not helping the community of Baltimore City when things like this are brought to light. But what I can say is I appreciate it being brought to light because seeing his transcript is not unusual to me. I've seen many transcripts, many report cards, like this particular student."

Dr. Santelises was Baltimore City Schools' CEO for all four years that France's son was a freshman. But she refused to interview with Project Baltimore when we broke this story. Instead, we received a two-page statement, which explains what *should* happen when a student is chronically absent or failing.

The district said students receive regular letters about their academic status, and records can be accessed through the campus portal. When a student is absent, an automated call is placed to the number on file. The statement also said the school conducts home visits. France says none of that happened. We later learned Augusta Fells had the wrong address and incorrect phone number for France.

What the statement from Santelises did not address was why France's son was promoted despite failing nearly two dozen classes. It didn't discuss his class rank or the 58 other students with a GPA of 0.13 or lower.

"It took a lot for me to just build the courage to do this," sobbed France during our interview. "He feels embarrassed, he feels like a failure."

During our interview with the administrator, I asked the employee what they would do if they could speak with France.

"I didn't have a handle on this student, but I worked for City Schools. So, he is one of my kids. I would hug her, and I would apologize profusely," replied the administrator.

By the end of our initial interview with France, she was a mess. My heart hurt for this mother. I had never interviewed anyone so lost. Her weeping eyes. Her trembling voice. Her depressed body language. Each individual aspect of her was crying out for help. I wanted to help her so badly.

"I'm like, [son], you can't feel like that. And you have to be strong, and you got to keep fighting. Life is about fighting. Things happen, but you got to keep fighting." She was emotionally exhausted. "And he's willing, he's trying, but who would he turn to when the people that's supposed to help him is not? Who do he turn to?"

* * *

That first Augusta Fells story aired on the evening of March 1, 2021, at 10:15. Almost immediately, calls for an investigation and for the school to be shut down began.

"I believe it's violating the constitutional rights of the children," said Clarence Mitchell, of the *C4 and Bryan Nehman* show on WBAL Radio. C4 stands for Clarence Mitchell IV. He's the grandson of a civil rights icon. On North Calvert Street in Baltimore stands the Clarence M. Mitchell Jr. Courthouse. "There is no way in the world you can look at what is being reported by Project Baltimore and say that they are providing those children with a thorough and efficient form of public education."

"That is astonishing. Absolutely astonishing. This school needs to be shut down," replied his co-host, Bryan Nehman. "If we have half the kids in the school that have below a 0.13. Not a 1.3, people. A 0.13, that school needs to be shut down. It's not doing its job."

"It's the agenda of the school system," replied C4. "I'm putting this right where it is, Bryan. The $17,000 they get per kid is gone if this kid leaves the system to get real help for his academic problems. They keep them moving to keep the money coming in."

Added Nehman, "They need to go to that school today and say, 'we need to see all the paperwork. We need to check everybody's records. We need to look at all of the grades and figure out what is going on here.'"

In the first 24 hours after Project Baltimore broke the story, our reporting received thousands of comments and shares, just on Facebook. And as C4 and Bryan Nehman were calling for an investigation, live on air, Rick Henry, Maryland's Inspector General for Education, wrote the show.

"The inspector general is listening to us right now," explained C4 on his show. "And based upon what we are sharing, he is asking that please anybody who knows anything about this story and other issues, please contact him."

"I'm glad he's listening, and I do hope people do call if they know anything about it or can give more information," stated Nehman.

But it wasn't just media personalities that had a strong reaction. Days after our first story, Maryland Governor Larry Hogan called for a full investigation.

"This is completely unacceptable," Hogan told me. We interviewed him outside his office in Annapolis. "It's worse than anything I've heard in the whole time that I've been governor. The fact that this particular school in the Baltimore City school system is failing that many kids is just outrageous."

By March 2021, Hogan was in his second term as governor. When he won re-election, he became the first Republican governor to win two terms in Maryland since the 1950s.

"I feel bad for this mom and this young man and the rest of the kids who haven't had the opportunity to get a quality education. If they are persistently failing schools, we have to shut the schools down. Or get rid of the principals and the teachers and start over with a new program.

We're failing the kids. That is what this is really all about," said the governor.

Hogan added, "There's no excuse for people ducking your questions. I don't have authority over the Baltimore City Schools, but I'm here talking to you. I think the entire school system needs to be held accountable. This school, the leaders of this school. The principal and the assistant principals. The superintendent and the school board all need to answer."

As we were interviewing Governor Hogan, Baltimore's mayor, Brandon Scott, was also talking about our investigation on the *C4 and Bryan Nehman* show on WBAL Radio. "We have to understand that these students need help. They don't need to be pushed through," he said.

"Mayor Scott," responded C4, "we have schools, and we knew about this because of Project Baltimore, that are literally failure factories, pushing kids grade to grade when they shouldn't be and creating, Mayor Scott, an underclass ward in our city."

"We know that we can no longer continue to educate our children the way that we have been, C4," continued the mayor. "What we can do and what I will do, from my position, having the influence of what we can do to improve those things and hold people accountable and not doing what has led so many families of being—putting out people who simply cannot succeed."

C4 jumped in, "Because they become future criminals, for the most part, you know that, Mr. Mayor."

Mayor Scott added, "Or victims, or victims, yep."

* * *

Long before our first story on this topic aired, we had been trying to track down Augusta Fells former principal Tracy Hicks. We didn't know too much about Hicks. Initially, we just wanted to ask her about France's son and the other 58 students in his class who had a grade point average near zero. She proved to be a difficult person to find. Especially since she no longer worked in a school.

North Avenue told us it also spotted "irregularities" at Augusta Fells and opened an internal investigation in 2019. At that time, Hicks and Augusta Fells' assistant principal, Joy Kwesiga, were placed on administrative leave. That is what North Avenue told us. What they failed to initially tell us is that Hicks and Kwesiga stayed on payroll that entire time—earning six figure salaries.

Once we learned this, we ramped up our efforts to locate Hicks, who had worked for City Schools for nearly 23 years. According to online records, she retired from City Schools in January 2021, two months before we broke the story. She had been on administrative leave for 17 months prior to retiring.

Based off her 2018 salary, in those 17 months, Hicks earned nearly $190,000. The assistant principal, Joy Kwesiga, still worked for City Schools when our story aired and was on paid administrative leave. Since City Schools' investigation into Augusta Fells began in the summer of 2019, Kwesiga earned $175,000.

Combined, taxpayers had paid about $370,000 to the administrators of Augusta Fells while they were on administrative leave. North Avenue told us in a statement that it's required by law to pay employees during an internal investigation—an investigation that ended up taking two years!

As Project Baltimore tried to contact Principal Hicks, we wrote her emails and called multiple phone numbers. We never heard back. We mailed her a letter, but still nothing. So, we went to Hanover, Pennsylvania, to her last known address, and knocked. No answer. One of her neighbors gave me her cell phone. I left a message and never heard back.

We felt this was too big a story not to include the other side. Why would a principal who is making a healthy six-figure salary do something to trigger such a massive scandal? What is the incentive?

No member of City Schools' leadership would interview with Project Baltimore to answer our questions. But the pressure was mounting. It was coming from all over the public and private spectrum. And that pressure forced Dr. Santelises to do something I had never seen a school superintendent do before. She apologized.

"I want to take this opportunity to apologize to those students and families who may be affected," said Dr. Santelises during the first school board meeting following our reporting on Augusta Fells. "We will continue to work with families on corrective steps to get students on the path to graduation."

A few days after Dr. Santelises issued that public apology, I interviewed a recent student at Augusta Fells, Marcus Turner.

"You heard that apology from Dr. Sonja Santelises?" I asked him.

"Yes, I have."

"When you heard that, what did you think?"

"It's not enough. It really isn't. It's not enough." Turner graduated from Baltimore City Schools in June 2020. "You can't apologize for years and years of people being held back. You can't apologize for people that don't do what they need to do in order to graduate because they don't deserve it."

That comment from Turner caught my attention. "In your time at Augusta Fells," I replied, "would you say that you saw students graduate who should not have graduated?"

He aggressively nodded, "Oh yes. Yes, most definitely."

Turner spent two years at Augusta Fells before transferring and graduating from another city high school. When we interviewed him in March 2021, he was a student at Saint Agnes Medical Center studying phlebotomy. Turner told me he felt for Tiffany France and her son. So did Turner's mother.

"No, I was not surprised," replied Diane Turner when I asked her about Augusta Fells. "I was not surprised at all. That's something I was waiting to happen."

Turner had seven children attend Augusta Fells. She said it was a good school, but around 2014, things began to change, according to the data. In 2013, the year prior, attendance at Augusta Fells stood at 72 percent with a graduation rate of 78 percent. Five years later (2018), attendance was down to 65 percent, with just 54 percent of students graduating. It was 2012 when the school got a new principal, Tracy Hicks.

"I did know her," said Diane. "She was a difficult woman to deal with. She was very difficult."

Diane had a child at Augusta Fells in 2019 when Hicks and Kwesiga were removed from the school. But she didn't hear it from North Avenue.

"Nope. Never, not one time. No email, no phone call, no nothing," explained Diane Turner. "They should have informed every single parent, every single one of them."

City and state lawmakers told Fox45 News they also were left in the dark about the failures of Augusta Fells and North Avenue's internal investigation, that is, until we reported it. But Marcus said he knew what was happening. He says he watched it every day for two years.

"If possible, do not send your child to Augusta Fells, it's not worth it," warned Marcus. I could tell he took no pride in saying these words. It hurt him. "It's really not worth it. And it's not worth them trying to get an education there and constantly struggling."

France took a lot of heat on social media. Many of the thousands of comments this story generated attacked her. Many people blamed her for not knowing about her son's grades and absences. And there is certainly merit to those claims.

There are multiple levels of failure here. There's the teenager who didn't do the work and skipped school. But most teenagers will do whatever adults allow.

France has culpability. But she also has three kids and three jobs as a single mom. That is not to say she doesn't carry blame. It is to say that someone in her position relies on a school system to do its job, which is the third level of blame.

As journalists, we often hold the government most accountable. Baltimore City Schools gets billions of dollars from taxpayers to educate students. In this case, that didn't happen.

* * *

"Experienced and transformational," that was how Baltimore City Schools had described the new principal of Augusta Fells Savage Institute. This principal was brought in during North Avenue's internal investigation of the school. Her job was to turn the school around. You may recall the new principal's name . . . Kamala Carnes.

In September 2019, a few years before we broke the Augusta Fells story, Principal Carnes was the focus of another Project Baltimore investigation into allegations of grade changing at her former school, Joseph C. Briscoe Academy. If you recall, we had spoken with former students and had transcripts that showed at least one graduate was absent or late 110 days during his senior year. Records show he failed science, a required class, with a 59. But his transcript says he got a D—and graduated. And we had that recording where you could hear what appears to be Briscoe administrators discussing changing the grade of a senior who failed.

Following that initial Project Baltimore report, North Avenue launched an internal investigation into alleged grade changing at Briscoe.

That investigation somehow took 18 months to complete. It wasn't finished until February 2021. But Carnes was hired in summer 2020 as the new principal of Augusta Fells.

What this means is, as Augusta Fells was under investigation for grading irregularities, City Schools brought in a new principal who was also under investigation for grading irregularities, which would not have a result for another seven months.

City Schools said in a statement placing Carnes at Augusta Fells was the "correct decision" as she is a "proven leader," stating that "her performance to date and the finding in the investigation justifies that appointment."

I pulled up ten other internal grade-changing investigations conducted by North Avenue prior to 2019. Nearly all of them took between two and five months to complete. The Briscoe investigation took a year and a half. By the time it ended, Carnes had already been principal of Augusta Fells for seven months.

City Schools explained in another statement that, "matters like these require extensive interviews, follow-up, review of documentary evidence, and written analysis." The statement also cited staffing shortages and COVID for the delay.

I mentioned this in an earlier chapter, but it's worth mentioning again. Of the school's 21 teachers at Briscoe, only six were interviewed according to the report. The teacher who gave Fox45 News the student transcripts and a second teacher whom we interviewed about the allegations said they never spoke to the investigator. The recording from inside the school was not even addressed in the report.

The Briscoe investigation found the allegation of "improper grade changing" against Carnes to be "unsubstantiated." But the investigator found the data to be "inconclusive" as to whether improper grade changing was happening at the school.

The story about Carnes' reassignment got a lot of people talking. Why would the school system assign a principal who's under investigation to a school that is also under investigation? The day after we posed that question, I received a phone call from a high-ranking official in Baltimore City Schools. I assured the person their identity would remain anonymous. But when I say, "high ranking," I mean, "very high ranking."

Throughout my career, these types of calls have been fairly common. There are plenty of people who work in positions of public sector power who see what's really going on. But they aren't interested in ruining their careers or becoming pariahs in their social circles. Their consciences simply guide them to pick up the phone and call a journalist to have an off-the-record conversation.

Our call was about 35 minutes, and we discussed a lot. But the call had one main theme. This person had gone to city schools. They now worked for city schools. This person explained that if all the students who should be held back were held back, the failure rate in the school system would be astronomical, and the dropout rate would skyrocket. The education climate that currently exists, according to this school employee, was not designed for the advancement of the students, but rather for the employment of the adults.

The more students who fail, according to this person, the fewer students remain in school. And enrollment determines funding. Thus, the primary goal of the school system is to keep students enrolled. The secondary goal is to educate them. That is not to say, according to the source, that many students don't get educated. But it is to say education is not the top priority; funding is.

I've heard all this before. But to hear someone who worked inside North Avenue tell me this was disheartening. It's one thing to think something may be true. It's another when someone who knows confirms it.

"You're on the right track. You're exposing the right things. But the school system will never make substantial changes because there's too much money at stake," the person explained. "That is why state and city elected leaders are not demanding that the school system improve. Think about it, Chris, you have proven in numerous schools that students are not being properly educated. How many adults have lost their jobs?"

* * *

Our investigation into Augusta Fells produced reports for two years. And the story kept getting crazier and crazier as we peeled back the layers of the onion. When we initially broke the story on Augusta Fells, many anonymous sources reached out to me. But one source stuck out, for obvious reasons.

Based on the emails we received from this particular source, I gathered that the "source" was a group of people who worked at Augusta Fells. To this day, I have never met them. I never spoke to them. I never learned their names.

But they explained to me, from a burner email account, that they didn't trust the internal investigation into Augusta Fells that North Avenue conducted. These employees at Augusta Fells (or, so I assumed) didn't trust their own school system. So, they began sending me information to prevent a possible district cover-up. Here is one story we aired using the information the source gave me. Below is how we wrote the original script.

((START SCRIPT))

((ANCHOR))

Tonight, Fox45 News finds that a school already under investigation for grading irregularities has more problems.

((ANCHOR))

Documents just obtained by Project Baltimore's Chris Papst show, Augusta Fells Savage in West Baltimore appears to have had ghost students on the roll—students you're paying to educate, who aren't really there.

((TAKE PACKAGE))

(Knock)

Project Baltimore went knocking on doors . . .

(Knock)

. . . looking for families of former students at Augusta Fells Savage Institute in West Baltimore.

Chris: "You're her dad?"

Parent 1: "Yes."

Chris: "Oh, you're her mother?"

Parent 2: (affirmative)

Chris: "So, you think he left the school system in 2017?"

Parent 3: "Something like that, yes."

Chris: "When she was living here, she wasn't going to school?"

Parent 4: "I don't remember her going to school."

Now, Fox45 News has obtained this document, from October 2019, which contains the names of 21 seniors at Augusta Fells. Sources tell us the school compiled the list of students who, while enrolled on paper, were not physically attending class; some hadn't for years. They're known by educators as ghost students.

(Stand up)

Chris Papst: Project Baltimore
"In Maryland, schools receive funding per student. The more students enrolled, the more money the school gets. City Schools gets nearly $16,000 per student every year. So, the question is . . . did North Avenue get taxpayer money to educate 21 students who were on the rolls of Augusta Fells, but were not actually attending the school? That would come out to $331,653 of your money to educate students who weren't there?"

Parent: "As far as 2019, she was going none at all—to be honest."

Fox45 News redacted the names of the students, but this document shows that two students enrolled at Augusta Fells in 2019 hadn't received a grade since the 2015/2016 school year, three years prior. Another four students enrolled in 2019 hadn't received grades since the 2016/2017 school year. One student spent five years in the ninth grade. And the school likely received funding for all of them.

Chris: "You're confident she was not in school in the fall of 2019. She was not there?"

Parent: "No."

One student spent five years just in the 12th grade. This student earned 44 credits in seven years at the school. You only need 21 to graduate. So, why keep the student on the roll? The document even says, "explanation needed???" And yet, that student appeared to still be on the rolls, likely being funded.

In 2019, Augusta Fells got $5.3 million from taxpayers to educate 434 students on paper, which would have included these seniors, where the recommendation for most of them is to be withdrawn.

City Schools declined an interview, but told Fox45 News the document we obtained was dated three months after North Avenue identified problems at the school and began an internal investigation. In a statement, City Schools said, "The investigation is reviewing how grades were awarded, enrollment and attendance activities, and credit recovery programs."

The statement went on to say North Avenue is "working diligently to complete this complex investigation and will take actions to ensure accountability and transparency . . ."

Chris: "Your neighbor, Tracy Hicks, did she move?"

Voice: "Yes."

Project Baltimore has tried to track down Augusta Fells former principal, Tracy Hicks, and former assistant principal, Joy Kwesiga.

Chris at Kwesiga's apartment complex: "Hi, my name is Chris Papst, I'm with Fox45 News. I'm looking for Joy Kwesiga."

Neither would speak with us. But we had questions about these 21 seniors. We then sent an email to their supervisor, Jacque Hayden. She also declined to speak with us. So, we attempted to speak with her at her home.

(Chris knocking on house door)

Voice from behind the front door: "What do you want?"

Chris: Hi, Ms. Hayden?

Voice: "No, wrong address. She don't live her."

Chris: Jacque Hayden does not live here?

Voice: "She does not live here."

Chris: Can you tell me where she lives?

Voice: "Can you get off my property, please?"

(Chris walking away)

We later received this email from Hayden stating, "Under no circumstance are you to ever come to my home or contact me. I am fully prepared to take legal action for trespassing and harassment should you come to my home or contact me."

((END PACKAGE))

That list of 21 potential ghost students was just the start of what the source gave us. And with each additional data dump, the situation for City Schools deteriorated.

"I know it's happening. It's more than a certainty. I know that it happens," said Carl Stokes, a former city council member and charter school operator in Baltimore. Stokes is a tall, soft-spoken Black man who has spent seven decades in Baltimore City. You may remember his name from an earlier chapter.

"It's an open secret, to be frank with you," stated Stokes. "It's an open secret that the system is very sloppy in its accounting. And so, it's an open secret that there are thousands of kids who are not coming to school every day who are still on the rolls."

You see, our Augusta Fells internal source didn't just give us the list of 21 students; we also got some of their transcripts. One student, whose name we concealed, started at Augusta Fells in 2013. The last credit that the student earned was in 2017. But two years later, in fall 2019, he was still on the rolls. In his final year at the school, he had one class listed in his transcripts, yearbook.

Another student started at Augusta Fells in 2015. The last credit he earned was during the 16/17 school year. But he was still on the rolls of Augusta Fells in the fall of 2019 with a 0.8 GPA. His class rank was 91 of 101.

"The fact that kids aren't getting an education in itself is corrupt. Let alone the switching of enrollment numbers or the dollars that are involved," added Stokes. "It's just rife with corruption at the upper levels of the school system."

Stokes said at his charter school, if a student did not show up for 60 days, the student was removed from the rolls. He says the only way to know the extent of enrollment problems is to conduct a full external audit of North Avenue's books, which City Schools had refused to request. And in Maryland, the only way an independent audit can be performed is if the school system requests it. In other words, a school system has to agree to an audit of itself. Can you imagine that standard being applied to any other organization?

"How do you fix it?" I asked Stokes in our interview.

"First," he replied. "You clean house upstairs. Upstairs is corrupt. Upstairs doesn't care. The Baltimore City Public Schools is the most racist institution in the city of Baltimore, the most racist institution. It's killing the lives of thousands of Black kids, poor kids, across the board, black, white, or brown. They don't care, except for the paychecks they get every two weeks."

* * *

Everything you've read so far in this chapter, and perhaps in this book, has led up to what you're about to read. We all have defining moments in our careers. This report is one of mine.

((START SCRIPT))

((ANCHOR))

Tonight, Project Baltimore tracks down a ghost student who attended a West Baltimore high school now under investigation.

((ANCHOR))

As Chris Papst explains, this student and 20 others were kept on the rolls even though it appears they stopped attending school. In this student's case, he hadn't been there for years.

((TAKE PACKAGE))

Ghost Student:
"I attended the school from 2014 up until 2017."

This man, now 22 years old, is a former student at Augusta Fells Savage Institute in West Baltimore.

Ghost Student:
"From basically the beginning of 2017, all the way up in 2019 or whenever it was going on . . . I signed up for no classes. I was dropped out, left the school. Didn't enroll back in the school or nothing."

His former school is caught up in a scandal; it is currently under an internal investigation by North Avenue for grading irregularities and enrollment issues.

Chris: "I'm going to show you your transcripts."

Ghost Student: "Ok. That's fine."

We wanted to speak with this man because his name appears on this list, obtained by Project Baltimore, of 21 seniors enrolled at Augusta Fells in 2019. These students were enrolled even though it appears they were not attending the school; some hadn't for years.

Ghost Student:
"Yeah, I know none of them classes. I never went."

Ghost students—as they're known by educators—can be used to inflate enrollment numbers and increase the tax dollars a school receives. These 21 possible ghost students would mean taxpayers likely paid North Avenue $331,653 to educate students who were not there. This student confirmed to Project Baltimore that he couldn't have been going to Augusta Fells in fall 2019, because he was in jail.

Ghost Student: "From August up until December."

Chris: "So from August to December of 2019, you were incarcerated?"

Ghost Student: "Yes."

Court records show, in August 2019, the then-20-year-old was arrested on drug distribution charges. But in October of that year, his name appeared on this list of students enrolled at Augusta Fells, even though he wouldn't be released from jail for another two months, in December 2019.

> **Chris:** You can't think of any reason why your name would be on the rolls of that school?
>
> **Ghost Student:** "No, not at all."

And the questions go back even further than that. This man said he stopped attending Augusta Fells long before his 2019 arrest. He told Project Baltimore he dropped out in early 2017. But for two more years, according to his transcripts, *someone* enrolled him in classes like Algebra II, College Readiness, and English IV.

> **Ghost Student:** "They never said I was enrolled, or they never reached out saying I had to come back, or anything."

City Schools receives $15,973 per student, every year, from taxpayers. Meaning, if this man stayed on the rolls of Augusta Fells two years after he dropped out, as records indicate, North Avenue would have received $31,946 to educate just this one student, who says that he wasn't there.

> **Ghost Student:** "As I can see in the transcripts, yeah, I'm basically a ghost student, but I didn't enroll in the classes or anything. I've been gone since 2017, buddy."

((END SCRIPT))

Think about that for a minute. For years, someone actively enrolls a student in a school without the student's knowledge. Someone even enrolled the student while he is sitting in a jail cell. Meanwhile, taxpayers are giving Baltimore City Schools tens of thousands of dollars to educate that student. Does that sound illegal to you?

* * *

The headlines produced by our Augusta Fells coverage were powerful. And over the summer of 2021, the situation got heated. Baltimore's City Council was all but forced to hold a virtual hearing concerning our coverage. The hearing didn't go well for the lawmakers.

City Schools CEO Dr. Sonja Santelises attended the hearing. The public was told she would be answering questions about Augusta Fells Savage, ghost students, grade changing—all of it. But it didn't happen. The Council members didn't come anywhere close to challenging her. It was like they were afraid to learn the truth. The topics of attendance, grading and principal qualifications were mentioned. But the Council stopped short of asking any real questions. And when the public attendees got a turn to speak, their questions were shut down.

"You cannot ask the CEO no question," announced Councilman Robert Stokes when he opened the hearing up to public comment.

"I think this City Council and what it's doing is a joke," said one resident.

"This makes no sense, just like the administration and the school board make no sense," yelled one caller who exploded with emotion upon learning she could not directly question her school's CEO. "Dr. Santelises, she is failing our children! She is failing them! But you have people calling in, and we seem to be the only ones who are upset."

The caller screamed so loudly her strained voice distorted the virtual microphones. "You all should have your hands up and be screaming at this woman. Because she is failing our children."

Another caller passionately added, "I'm sitting here, and my heart is breaking for Baltimore and the future of Baltimore, mainly because this seems like a back-scratching session for each other."

We later learned *why* Council members may not have challenged Santelises. We obtained an email through a public records request that showed before the hearing, City Schools sent City Council members what it called "talking points" to combat Fox45's coverage. The "talking points" memo stated, "Given that many of you are receiving questions regarding the recent news story that aired on Fox45's Project Baltimore about a student in the ninth grade at Augusta Fells Savage, we are writing to provide talking points."

The memo listed a series of questions that Council members may get from the media. City Schools then guided the elected officials on how to answer those questions.

Here's an example:

Question: What is the current status [of the investigation]?

Answer: AFS (Augusta Fells Savage) continues to follow up with parents of students identified as needing support through the transcript review process. In addition, AFS continues to review student transcripts for concerns and directly contact students' parents to discuss any challenges.

The Maryland Public Policy Institute is a government watchdog group. Sean Kennedy is a Visiting Fellow, meaning he contributes his expertise to the group on a temporary basis. "The idea that the city schools are trying to control the narrative and expect that the City Council was going to tow their line should be very concerning to not only the residents of Baltimore and the City Schools parents, but everybody in Maryland. Because they are effectively trying to control the people who should have oversight over them."

Also in the summer of 2021, multiple rallies were staged calling for the school CEO to resign or face a class action lawsuit. The plaintiffs would be the parents and students who say they've been failed by their own school system. The rallies were not huge—maybe 30 people. But they marked a significant turning point. Frustration and angst were mounting. And much of it centered around the community learning damning information about their school system—not from their school system, but rather from the media.

"The school board has failed us and continues not to hold Santelises responsible," stated one rally participant, Jason Rodriguez.

"When one child fails, we all fail, and right now we have failed a lot of children," added Yolanda Pulley, another rally attendee.

These rallies were pretty standard. The 30 participants huddled in a group, holding signs and chanting the obligatory rhythmic chants: "No education, no peace. Resign now, Dr. Santelises. No education, no peace. Resign now, Dr. Santelises."

Many of the signs displayed at the rallies had misspellings. One young man, who appeared to be in elementary school, held a sign that said, "I am a Produce of Baltmore City SHcool!!"

"This is not a negotiation, the people elected will no longer be able to hold our children hostage," shouted protester Shannon Wright, who ran for mayor in 2020.

The heated summer of 2021 certainly cleared the way for what was coming that fall. All the pressure and news coverage seemed to work. In the fall, Baltimore City Schools was nearing completion of its internal investigation into Augusta Fells. And it released a summary report of the findings.

By this time, Project Baltimore had been reporting on Augusta Fells for six months. For all of those six months, City Schools downplayed our findings. They dismissed our work and, at times, disparaged it. But when North Avenue was forced to release the results of its own internal investigation, it confirmed most everything we had reported. The findings substantiated serious allegations of corruption involving grade changing and inflated enrollment.

The report cited three major findings: First, administrators at Augusta Fells improperly changed grades and pressured teachers to give students grades they did not earn. According to the report, some students may have earned the credits necessary to graduate based on those improper grades.

The second major finding from the report is that students were scheduled in classes that did not exist and/or that they did not attend, when they should have been withdrawn due to lack of attendance. The report says approximately 100 students had questionable status and may not have been actively attending school while still remaining on the rolls.

The third finding showed that the school was offering credit recovery programs, like summer school, for students to make up classes. But they didn't meet city school requirements.

The report says four people were implicated for their roles in the scheme. They included the principal and assistant principal, who, remember, collected nearly $400,000 in salary as City Schools conducted its investigation.

CEO Dr. Santelises released a statement concerning the findings: "The breach of trust by those former employees cannot be overstated. We are disappointed those adults would place their selfish motives above the well-being of students. While our systems worked to uncover the scheme, we also learned lessons that will lessen the chance this can happen again."

You may think that at this point, the story is over. Fox45 News uncovered a scandal. And City Schools' own investigation confirmed the reporting. But this storyline was far from over. The biggest headlines were yet to come.

* * *

How about this for a headline?

Taxpayers Fund $92 Million to Educate Missing Maryland Students in 2019

We ran that story in the fall of 2021. We assumed Augusta Fells was not alone. Our sources were telling us it was common practice for schools to add students to their enrollment to get more funding. They could do this, according to our sources, in a number of ways. But the most common was simple; if a student is enrolled in your school and leaves, you just keep them on the rolls. Students can move, drop out, pass away or go to jail. But if the school does not unenroll them, the school continues to get money for them.

In Maryland, a school's enrollment is based on the number of students enrolled on paper on September 30th. All funding is based on enrollment on that one day. But we found millions of dollars were being spent to educate students who later went missing.

Every year, the Maryland State Department of Education releases reports on students who are unenrolled. In 2019 (the most recent year available when we produced this report in 2021), 9,822 Maryland students left public school, some due to illness, lack of interest, or employment. But the largest category, with 6,126 students, is "whereabouts unknown." More than 6,000 students went missing. At around $15,000 each, Maryland schools received $92,796,648 in just one year to educate students that, according to state data, could not be found.

The Maryland State Department of Education declined an interview to discuss the funding of missing students but told me over the phone that school districts create yearly budgets based on their September 30 enrollment. If a student goes missing after September 30, the school still gets the money for that student, according to the education department, because the money was budgeted.

Baltimore City Schools told Fox45 News in a statement, it does attempt to find students with phone calls and home visits. If those attempts fail, and the student did not enroll in another school, they are labeled "whereabouts unknown."

When we reported these numbers, Republican State Delegate Kathy Szelga said the September 30th date creates an incentive that encourages fraud. She believes schools like Augusta Fells can pad enrollment, secure extra funding and later unenroll students, if necessary, by labeling them "whereabouts unknown" with few to no questions asked from the state.

"The whole system seems to be based on the wrong metrics," said Szeliga. "We need to base funding of students on them getting to school and those students getting education, and not just the fact that they were enrolled and showed up one time in September."

Then-State Comptroller, Peter Franchot, a Democrat, agreed with Szeliga.

"It's unacceptable for taxpayers' money to go for students that are knowingly not in the school system," said Franchot. "The fact that we're funding students whose whereabouts are unknown, and not a small number, thousands, and it adds up to tens of millions of dollars, that's something that needs to be looked at."

Franchot explained that to fix the problem, the state must change the way schools are funded. He suggested tying school funding to attendance.

"It's a very simple solution instead of taking one tally on September 30th, to see who's in school and who's out of school, they need to do it monthly," he said. "What we're doing now is just tragic, because we're committing the state in a direction where we know the kids that are graduating don't have the skill, the knowledge, or the self-confidence to independently take advantage of the free enterprise system."

* * *

March 2022 marked one year since we first interviewed Tiffany France. And in that one year, as you just read, a lot happened. So, we sat down with her again for a follow-up interview. We spoke about the fallout over the Augusta Fells scandal, the online beating she took as a mother, and how her life has changed. Local news doesn't always do this type of "follow-up" interview. I'm glad we did.

It's still incredible to me that our entire coverage of Augusta Fells started with one phone call from a mother worried about her son's education. And that one call would expose a massive scheme to change grades and inflate enrollment at the West Baltimore high school. And that mother who came forward saw her life turned upside down. Now, one year later, she says, she'd do it all again.

When we met France for our follow-up interview, she had moved to a new place. A much nicer place. She needed a fresh start. France had spent the entire previous year putting her life back together.

"I'm so glad all of this is over," she told me. "It was hard, it was hard for me, I had to motivate him, some days I didn't feel motivated to even tell him to get up. I just was like, 'I just don't care.' But I knew that I had to keep pushing him, and we did it, and I say, we, because this was a fight for both of us. Like, we did it."

When we spoke with France, it was nearly one year to the day since she made a decision that changed her life. She picked up the phone and called Fox45 News.

Because the facts are so outrageous, let's take a moment to review. France was in a bad place. She'd just learned her son, Christopher, had passed only three classes in four years at Augusta Fells Savage in West Baltimore. He had a 0.13 GPA and was still in ninth grade. With a class rank of 62 out of 120, he was being promoted through the course levels. That led France to believe everything was fine when it wasn't.

France didn't know it then, but her story would set off a six-month Project Baltimore investigation that exposed serious issues in City Schools, from grade changing to padding enrollment.

The fallout was enormous. France's story went viral, collecting millions of pageviews while igniting outrage at the highest levels in the state, including from Governor Larry Hogan, who publicly stated, "This is completely unacceptable. It's worse than anything I've heard in the whole time that I've been governor."

"I felt like I was in somebody else's life," said France, speaking of all the publicity. "It was just really different for me; it was so many people contacting me."

But as the story grew, France watched the backlash turn to her. Hundreds of comments on social media questioned her decisions as a single parent.

She responded to the critics, "I had went through a divorce, and that was us finding our way back, so trying to figure out a new life for us, and I felt bad every day that Christopher had to even go to that school."

France has two younger children. When the reports began airing, she was working multiple jobs, trying to stay afloat. The criticism was difficult to read.

"It was so many people saying so many things that was just so cruel, like online, about him and me, that was just completely not true." As France spoke, she wasn't emotional or upset. She was just calmly explaining her experience. I detected no animosity or antipathy in her delivery. It appeared France had come to peace with her reality.

Somehow, France was able to tune out the negativity and turn inward, focusing on getting her son out of Augusta Fells and into a mentoring program.

"I told him this is not how the story is going to end," she declared.

And it wasn't. Six months after Project Baltimore broke this story, an internal investigation by City Schools confirmed a massive scheme to inflate enrollment and change grades at Augusta Fells. France's son was a victim.

Now, four employees, including the principal and vice principal, were implicated and no longer work for City Schools. Local and state agencies launched additional investigations. And a bill was introduced in Annapolis to change how Maryland schools are funded.

"The story, by being so big, I think that it pushed Christopher to prove people wrong," France asserted. "It made him fight more."

France's son enrolled in an accelerated diploma program at a new Baltimore City school with new teachers and new leadership; he thrived.

France gave me a copy of her son's report card. "These are his final grades for the first semester. A-, B+, C+, B, A, A+, C." I paused and then looked up at her with a smile. "Those are good grades."

"Yeah." This mom was finally happy.

Christopher was on track to graduate. He said, at the time, he hoped to go to college.

"He's been doing exceptionally well. I'm so proud of him, honestly." France was beaming.

Before our interview was over, I asked France one final question. "After all of this, after everything has happened with you and your son, what is your opinion of Baltimore City Schools?"

The words came quickly. "They need a lot of help. They need a whole lot of help. These kids aren't prepared for life, they're just not."

Through her entire ordeal, France had grown as a mother and an advocate for her children and others.

"I felt helpless in this process, and I think there's a lot of parents that may feel helpless, they feel overwhelmed," she concluded. "I am 100% proud that I stood up and spoke up."

* * *

That follow-up report on Tiffany France was our final "personal" story in this series. Tiffany and her son blew the whistle on something they knew was wrong, but didn't fully understand. We were then able to take the pieces she gave us and assemble the parts to uncover a massive scandal. Based on our website page views, many people around the country were following this story. But for many Maryland lawmakers, there was nothing to see.

Maryland has a part-time legislature. Each year, starting in January, legislators meet in Annapolis for 90 days. All the legislative work each year is completed in those 90 days. The Democratic Party controls both the Senate and the House.

In January of 2022, our work on Augusta Fells motivated one Republican lawmaker to take action.

"To me, the education of our children is a bipartisan issue," explained Delegate April Rose, who represents Carroll County.

Rose introduced House Bill 1365 before the House Appropriations Committee. To create more accurate enrollment counts, and thus distribute taxpayer money more accurately to schools, Rose's bill required schools to count enrollment four times a year. Funding would then be based on the average of the four counts.

"It's not that hard to count kids. All I'm asking is for four times a year," stated Rose concerning her bill. "We need to make sure we are spending taxpayer money wisely and fairly, and certainly getting the return on that investment. That is correct and fair to everyone."

Bills that impact school funding are generally hotly debated in Annapolis. When Rose went before the Appropriations Committee to present the bill, she expected pushback. To her surprise, she didn't get any.

"We must get this right for our kids and our taxpayers," Rose told the Committee. "In addition to fixing the problem of taxpayer money not being spent properly, we must also do a better job of finding out why these children are not in school."

When Rose was done, she waited for questions from the Committee members.

"Are there any questions from the Appropriations Committee for Delegate Rose?" Asked the Committee Vice Chair.

Complete silence. No questions. No Opposition. No anything. Her hearing lasted two minutes.

So, what happened? Rose's bill was intended to save taxpayer dollars, potentially millions of dollars every year, going to educate students who aren't in school. But Rose's bill wasn't supported or opposed; it was ignored.

Project Baltimore did some digging. We learned that, before Rose presented House Bill 1365, three written statements from very powerful political groups were sent to the Committee; all three opposed the bill.

The Maryland State Education Association, the state's largest teachers' union, wrote that the bill "overcomplicates a data snapshot that is intended to ensure adequate funding for schools."

Howard County Public Schools called the bill a "different variation of the current problem," saying enrollment would still be based on snapshots in time and school budgets could be delayed if the average enrollment isn't calculated until the end of the school year.

Anne Arundel County Public Schools wrote that this bill could reduce their funding, and they "oppose any revenue reductions."

Rose says the Maryland teachers' union has so much power, as soon as they opposed the bill, it was effectively dead, which is why she believes the Committee ignored her.

"It was absolutely done to save taxpayers' money," Rose explained of her bill. "But again, I don't want to put aside, if we've got kids that are in jail and not in school, clearly what we're doing now, the status quo of what we've been doing, is not working."

You may have noticed, when Rose presented her bill, it was the Vice Chair, not the Chair of the committee, who solicited questions. Where was the Chair? Why wasn't the Chair leading the hearing? The simple answer is: because she wasn't there. She left the meeting shortly before Rose presented her bill. So, for the next few days, we tried to find out why.

In January 2022, the Chair of the Maryland House Appropriations Committee was Maggie McIntosh. Her district included Baltimore City. McIntosh looks like your stereotypical grandmother, short and round, with white hair and dense glasses. She had been a member of Maryland's General Assembly for decades. And the Democrat had no interest in speaking with me about House Bill 1365.

I repeatedly emailed and called McIntosh's office trying to learn why she left the Appropriations meeting before Rose presented her school enrollment bill.

But similar to Rose, I was also being ignored. So, I went to the State House (Maryland's Capitol) when I knew Delegate McIntosh was in session on the floor. I waited patiently for her to leave the chamber during a recess, and then I politely approached her with a mic and a cameraman, of course.

"Hi, Delegate McIntosh. My name is Chris Papst with Fox45 News."

McIntosh stopped and looked up at me. Those around her stepped away from the camera. McIntosh was on her way to another meeting. I didn't have a lot of time.

Amongst the glory of the State House's veined marble walls and columns, I immediately pulled out a copy of House Bill 1365 and showed it to McIntosh.

"This is House Bill 1365," I stated.

McIntosh looked down at the bill in wide-eyed ignorance. I didn't even get out a question before she started to respond.

"I don't . . ." she stuttered. "I'm totally," she stuttered more, "I mean, I'd love to talk with you about it when I read the bill."

When I heard those last five words, I almost fell over.

"You never read the bill?" I asked in utter disbelief. I thought perhaps I didn't hear her correctly. "But it came before your committee."

She didn't miss a beat.

"I was negotiating on the tax package with the governor, so I wasn't at the hearing. And I don't read every bill."

That's verbatim what she said.

House Bill 1365 was created to safeguard tax dollars—potentially tens of millions of tax dollars. But McIntosh had no interest. She hadn't even bothered to read it.

At this point, McIntosh must have thought our interview was over. She just walked away from me and went outside. So, I followed her.

"Are you familiar with Augusta Fells?" I asked, just to make sure I fully understood her position. At this point, we were outside, walking down the steps at the front of the State House. My photographer scrambled out of the large wooden doors and quickly circled down the stairs to capture our conversation.

"I am not," she replied.

I was now even more stunned.

Our reports on Augusta Fells received millions of views on FoxBaltimore.com. Dr. Santelises issued a public apology to parents at the school. The Maryland Inspector General for Education publicly announced an investigation. Maryland's Governor and Comptroller both made public statements calling what happened at Augusta Fells "unacceptable." I mean, a piece of legislation was drafted based on the Augusta Fells scandal and presented before the Committee she chairs. Yet, McIntosh, who represented parts of Baltimore City, said she never heard of it. How is that possible?

"Sorry," she replied as we continued our walk down the State House stairs, "television folks are not the ones I listen to about bills."

"Well," I replied, "you don't have to listen to me, the bill is right here." I tried to hand her my copy of the bill as we walked. "I can give it to you if you'd like to see it."

Again, she had no interest.

We were now crossing the street towards the House of Delegates building. My photographer was in front of us, backpaddling and trying not to run into anything or anyone. The 90-day session is a busy time. There were lawmakers, lobbyists, tourists, state employees, and students on field trips all around us.

"I will be in touch with your office," I said to McIntosh as she approached the door of her office building.

"They'd be very happy to hear from you." She tried to act sincerely.

I got the feeling she didn't mean that. But either way, I held the door for her as she stepped inside the building. "I hope we hear back from you on this bill. I appreciate your time."

A few hours later, McIntosh apparently found time to read House Bill 1365. That afternoon, her committee met for a hearing. And this time, she was present.

"I looked at this bill," she announced, "because I was asked to look at it just recently."

In her comments, McIntosh opposed the bill, saying a few isolated incidents of inflated enrollment do not justify the legislation. But she also said the state board of education should look into the issue.

When the vote happened, House Bill 1365 died. But the Augusta Fells scandal would simply not go away.

* * *

((BEGIN SCRIPT))

((ANCHOR))

A bombshell report confirms millions of tax dollars are being misallocated statewide—to educate students who aren't even in school.

((ANCHOR))

As Project Baltimore's Chris Papst explains, an audit by the Inspector General for Education found many Maryland schools have been miscalculating attendance and enrollment . . . costing taxpayers at least 23 million dollars.

((TAKE PAPST))

This audit follows a Fox45 investigation into so-called ghost students, who are kept on the rolls to increase the amount of funding a school receives. And according to this new IG report, it's an issue that's been costing taxpayers millions across the state for years.

((TAKE PACKAGE))

Sean Kennedy: MPPI
"Taxpayers in Maryland were cheated, and the fraud needs to stop."

Sean Kennedy is with the Maryland Public Policy Institute. In April 2021, the non-profit sent a request to Maryland's Inspector General for Education asking the office to investigate enrollment discrepancies.

Sean Kennedy: MPPI
"It's a big deal that we are catching them spending money that they should not have had."

The request followed a series of Project Baltimore reports on ghost students who are not attending class but are kept on the rolls to increase the funding a school receives. In 2021, Fox45 News learned of 21 potential ghost students enrolled at Augusta Fells in West Baltimore, including a student who was enrolled while in jail.

((File: 4/21)) **Ghost Student:**
"I didn't enroll in the classes or anything. I've been gone since 2017, buddy."

An internal investigation by City Schools confirmed the problem was worse than we knew, finding approximately 100 students with questionable enrollment status at just this one school. Now, we know the problem is even bigger.

Sean Kennedy: MPPI
"This is nothing less than theft. They're stealing money from the taxpayers of Maryland in order to line their pockets or to spend money on other programs when the money was not designated for that."

The IG's audit looked at enrollment counts over the last five years and found 928 instances of students in just Baltimore City alone who did not meet attendance or enrollment requirements under Maryland law. 532 Baltimore City students didn't have any recorded attendance during the year.

Those students should not have been eligible for funding, but City Schools received $10 million in taxpayer dollars to educate those students who were not there.

In the same five-year period, the IG found nearly 3,000 instances of students statewide who should not have received funding, including 995 students who had no documented attendance at any point during the year. That adds up to nearly $24 million in misallocated tax dollars.

The report blames these errors on poor attendance keeping and staff not withdrawing chronically absent students. But it also says over 92% (2,757) of the discrepancies were discovered and self-reported to the Maryland State Department of Education, which "did not identify or act on these discrepancies during the reporting process . . ."

Sean Kennedy: MPPI
"The inspector general found out this is the tip of the iceberg."

The report says there are "more discrepancies" statewide concerning students who are funded and should not be, meaning the problem is bigger than nearly $24 million over five years. But no word on how much bigger. To fix the problem, however large, the audit offers nine total recommendations between City Schools and MSDE to help ensure a more accurate enrollment count. North Avenue and MSDE have agreed to implement most of them.

Sean Kennedy: MPPI
"It's unclear if it was intentional as an outright fraud or if this was just sloppy bookkeeping that happened to benefit them. There was no interest in providing oversight when that oversight would have cost that money. So, they let egregious bookkeeping go on because it always came out in their favor."

((TAG: PAPST))

It's important to note that this audit only focused on students who should not have been eligible to receive funding. We found more than 6,000 students statewide in 2019 labeled "whereabouts unknown." Even though those students went missing throughout the year, the IG says, most of them were still eligible to receive funding under Maryland law, costing taxpayers millions of dollars.

((END SCRIPT))

When the IG released his report, I recalled Delegate McIntosh's reason for voting against House Bill 1365. "A few isolated incidents of inflated enrollment do not justify the legislation," she said. Apparently, saving taxpayers AT LEAST $24 million isn't worth voting for a bill, or even reading it. The inspector general said the problem was much larger than what he found.

It makes you wonder, how much money would a bill have to save taxpayers before she'd consider supporting it?

* * *

Over the next few months, not much happened with Augusta Fells. No news. No updates. No anything. The wheels of government certainly turn slowly. But eighteen months after we first broke the Augusta Fells story, we learned taxpayers got some money back.

According to the Maryland State Department of Education, City Schools was forced to refund the state $350,517 for 73 students over a five-year period, who were enrolled and funded at Augusta Fells when they should not have been.

"I was actually happy that was occurring because they took our report seriously," Rick Henry, Maryland's Inspector General for Education, said to me. "We feel it's a problem and we've identified it as a problem."

Henry did not investigate the motivation behind the inflated enrollment at Augusta Fells. City Schools had told us in a statement what happened at Augusta Fells was "a coordinated scheme" by four employees, "none of whom is still employed by City Schools."

As part of his report, the inspector general issued recommendations to have more accurate counts, which included removing unenrolled students who drop out within ten days. City Schools publicly stated it implemented those recommendations.

With those new measures in place, we then looked at City Schools enrollment numbers the following year in 2023. Enrollment fell by 1,812 students to just under 76,000 (75,995). The largest one-year drop in the previous 16 years. Coincidence?

Baltimore City Schools Enrollment

2023: 75,995 (down 1,812)
2022: 77,807
2021: 77,856
2020: 79,187
2019: 79,297
2018: 80,591
2017: 82,354
2016: 83,666
2015: 84,976
2014: 84,730
2013: 84,747
2012: 84,212
2011: 83,800
2010: 82,866
2009: 82,266
2008: 81,284
2007: 82,381

No one was ever charged criminally for what happened at Augusta Fells. Even though it appears more than $350,000 was stolen from taxpayers.

There were also the other students throughout the state that the IG said were funded when they should not have been. What happened to all that money? It totaled tens of millions of dollars.

The Maryland State Department of Education told me in a statement: "MSDE has not collected any funds from (other school systems) as a result of the OIGE's report. Notwithstanding the report on Augusta Fells Savage, MSDE has no reason to believe any local education agency in Maryland intentionally and systematically inflates attendance for the purposes of collecting State aid."

This is mind-blowing.

Remember what *McDonalds* said, "*Everything* is about data. And data is money."

Enrollment counts are data, directly tied to per-pupil funding. You would think the state would mandate and expect enrollment counts to be highly accurate. Instead, sloppy bookkeeping is permitted, which results in millions of dollars being misappropriated to schools.

And when there is an intentional "scheme" (City Schools' word) to inflate enrollment to collect more funding, no one is charged with a crime. Sure, some people lost their jobs, but only after receiving hundreds of thousands of dollars in pay while on administrative leave.

Think about that for a second.

Billions of dollars are up for grabs in public education funding. And it appears schools are incentivized to shake down taxpayers to collect more of it. If educators get caught intentionally inflating enrollment, they don't go to jail. And if schools keep sloppy books, which results in additional funding, the errors are excused.

Welcome to Baltimore. For that matter, welcome to Maryland.

CHAPTER 14

12,542

June 7, 2022. The day I got the text. One word. Six letters. All it said was,
"posted." It was a text for which I had been waiting years. Four years, ten
months and five days to be exact.

That is how long it had been since we published our first story on
improper grade changing inside Baltimore City Schools. Four years, ten

months and five days over which we produced around 100 total reports, took the district to court, and read through thousands of emails from school employees. Four years, ten months and five days in which we heard from, spoke with, or interviewed hundreds of concerned parents, students and teachers who said students were being cheated out of the education they deserved. Four years, ten months and five days where City Schools denied our reporting, calling it sensational and inaccurate.

Rick Henry is Maryland's Inspector General for Education. And he looks the part: stoic, bald and around 60 years old. By the time his office was created by the Maryland legislature in 2020, we were three years deep in our grade-changing investigation. Apparently, he had been watching. Because when he started the job, one of the first investigations his office launched was in response to our investigation. Two years later, he released his findings. And they were explosive.

"I think it's a big deal." The day after Henry released his report, he interviewed with Project Baltimore. "The allegations are very strong. And, you know, to pass students along or just round up the grades, it does a disservice. If you're setting them up for failure, this is a way of doing it."

The IG's report was 29 pages long. It cites Project Baltimore's reporting that "alleged grades were being improperly changed at some schools to inflate student achievement and reduce rates of failure and retention. BCPS (Baltimore City Public Schools) described the report as having possible mischaracterizations, inaccuracies and sensationalism."

Here are the highlights of the report. The IG focused on 136 Baltimore City Schools, grades 6-12. He only looked at four school years, 2016-2020. In that time period, his office found that 12,542 failing grades were improperly changed to passing. That is not a typo, 12,542. Henry's office estimated that up to 10% of students at some schools graduated who should not have. Baltimore City Schools generally has the lowest graduation rate in Maryland, which usually hovers around 70%. And the IG found that the number has been inflated due to grade changing.

"A number of the teachers, a number of the educational professionals, felt as though they were pressured to make changes. And our team actually showed that this was occurring," Henry told me. "What was very stunning to us is that we were being told—by the school system—that this was not the practice. But we were seeing it as we were looking through all of the documents that were provided by the city schools. We kept uncovering more and more."

Similar to the emails we obtained through our lawsuit against City Schools, the IG's report includes several examples of emails where teachers were told to change failing grades to passing. And they were not shy about it. One email from an assistant principal at Digital Harbor High School reads, "Per principal, all 58s and 59s must be changed to a 60."

You can't get more direct than that.

Another email sent to an assistant principal at Mergenthaler High School reads, "Please change the following students' progress from failing to passing." No shame. No hiding it.

I asked the IG if these 12,542 grade changes could be earned. Perhaps the student did extra work or retook a test. He told me he removed those examples. The 12,542 only included grade changes that were not accompanied by a legitimate reason.

So now, after nearly five years, our reporting had been confirmed. City Schools could no longer deny it. The question then became, where did that directive to change grades come from? If we have emails from principals telling their staff to change failing grades to passing, were those principals being pressured by North Avenue? As part of the investigation, the IG's office interviewed the CEO, Dr. Sonja Santelises, and the Chief of Schools, John Davis. And both made a stunning claim. When we read the report for the first time, we couldn't believe it.

Dr. Santelises told investigators she was "unaware of undue pressure on principals to change grades."

Davis told investigators he didn't have "any evidence" that North Avenue was pressuring principals to change grades.

Seriously?!

Most everything you've read over the last fourteen chapters was literally televised, posted on Fox45's website and blasted all over social media. Our reports have received millions of pageviews. So have our social media accounts.

I understand the CEO and the Chief of Schools have likely not watched every Project Baltimore report. They may not have seen the report cards, student transcripts, emails and text messages that proved improper grade changing was happening on a mass scale. Perhaps, they didn't see the teachers who spoke with us on camera, saying they were pressured to pass failing students. Maybe, just maybe, the CEO and Chief of Schools didn't pay close attention when Fox45 sued the district and won in court.

But how could the two highest-ranking officials at North Avenue claim to be "unaware" when, in 2019, I told them about it in person? Remember, when I signed up for public comment and spoke at the school board meeting? Dr. Santelises and John Davis were at that board meeting. They were in the room when I said directly to them, "Grade changing is happening at Baltimore City Public Schools."

To claim they were unaware of any pressure on principals is stunning. It's just one reason why many people in Baltimore have lost trust and faith in their own school system. It's also why many people feel Baltimore City Schools will never significantly improve.

How can you fix a problem of which you claim to be unaware?

And it's a problem, Henry said, that is likely even bigger than we realize.

"Our report only touched the surface," he said. "And I think there's more there. We were relying upon Baltimore City to turn over the documents that we were asking for, and we based our report on those documents that the city themselves turned over to us."

Concerning his office's subpoena power, he said, "You're only as good as what the agency turns over to you."

In his report, the IG describes, "A culture of fear and a veil of secrecy affected the BCPS system that kept many from speaking freely about misconduct." To understand the scope of the problem, Henry recommended an emergency, independent audit of city schools' grading practices to be conducted between the years 2016 and 2020.

But in Maryland, in order for that audit to happen, the local school system would have to agree to it (it's worth continuing to point that out). And City Schools did not agree to it. The district said it may consider an audit of the 2022-2023 school year. But not the years when Henry found 12,542 failing grades changed to passing.

"To me, it would show that they're continuing the same practice now, in this particular school year, and they're waiting for a school year when they can improve their numbers," Henry hypothesized.

In the wake of the IG's findings, public officials across the state began calling for a criminal investigation into grade changing, including then-Governor Larry Hogan.

In a letter to the state prosecutor, Hogan said, "The report reveals egregious behavior by Baltimore City Public Schools employees, which, if proven true in a court of law, would seem to constitute criminal malfeasance in certain cases."

The fallout from the IG's report was intense. The calls for a criminal investigation and for the CEO, Dr. Sonja Santelises, to resign were heavily echoed outside Baltimore. But inside city limits, the response was very different.

And recall, in 2019, following Project Baltimore's initial reporting, City Schools passed a new grade-changing policy, which included additional training for grade reporters and required principals to notify teachers in writing before student grades are adjusted. But did it work? Apparently, not.

According to the IG's report, at least 3,000 of the 12,542 improper grade changes occurred AFTER the 2019 policies were put in place. In response to the IG findings, the Maryland State Department of Education requested that City Schools provide an overview of its grading policy and create a plan to ensure grades are accurate.

The district responded. Starting in the 2022/2023 school year, North Avenue announced new checks and balances so that "no single school staff person is solely responsible for any aspect of the grading entry." Grade reporters must now be "certified instructional employees." As far as the rounding of grades, there's a clear line. A decimal of 0.4 and lower is rounded down, 0.5 or more is rounded up. So, a failing grade of 59.5 will automatically be rounded up to a passing grade of 60.

UPDATE: City Schools did perform an audit of its grading system for the 2022/2023 school year. The district hired its own auditors, strictly controlled the parameters of the audit, and refused to allow the media access to the process. The district's auditors found four improper grade changes that year. Yes . . . four.

The IG found 12,542 improper grade changes over four years. When City Schools hired its own auditors, they only found four. And when the auditors presented their findings to the school board during a public meeting in early 2024, the district denied the media access to the auditors. We were not allowed to ask the auditors questions about the audit. I wonder why.

* * *

July 5, 2022: Four weeks after the IG's report was released and five years after we first began reporting on grade fixing in City Schools.

If you've never been to Baltimore City Hall, you should visit. The rotunda is remarkable. Rising 119 feet above a polished marble floor, the dome is capped with stained glass, twisted metal and meticulously detailed plaster. Built in 1867, it's another symbol of the wealth, power and prestige that Baltimore once possessed, similar to the district headquarters at North Avenue.

"Good morning, everyone," announced Baltimore Mayor Brandon Scott. The 38-year-old mayor was half encircled by elected city leaders, school board members and the School CEO, Dr. Santelises. "Thank you for joining us for this special, special moment today. We are celebrating someone who doesn't get celebrated enough, if it was up to me."

On this day, July 5th, the media had gathered for what was billed as a summer learning event. I did not attend. But I wish I had. Because it turns out, the event was not about educating students.

Mayor Scott, a proud graduate of Baltimore City Public Schools, had called everyone to the rotunda to mark a milestone. The City Schools CEO had just completed her sixth year, making her the second-longest tenured superintendent in Baltimore City Schools' nearly 200-year history. This event was a surprise celebration in her honor.

"You've encountered a number of challenges over the last few years," explained Mayor Scott, speaking to a stunned Santelises, "a budget deficit that resulted in layoffs, regular criticism from local media." He paused to emphasize, "*That* should be bolded."

Scott then listed some of Dr. Santelises' accomplishments, which mostly included her success in constructing new school buildings during her tenure.

"She didn't know this press conference was happening," chuckled Maryland Senate President Bill Ferguson, who represents Baltimore

City. Ferguson is a former high-ranking administrator in city schools. In congratulating Santelises, he spoke about the importance of longevity. "What really matters when you look across the country, stability is what matters," he said.

Delegate McIntosh (you know, the Committee Chair who had never heard of Augusta Fells) was there. In her short speech, she just joked, saying, "Thank you very much (Dr. Santelises) for the *next* six years of your life." Everyone behind her burst out in laughter.

State Senator Cory McCray simply affirmed with immense pride, "We have the right leader."

What was oddly missing from any of these joyous speeches was Dr. Santelises' record on student achievement. When looking at any school system, the performance metrics politicians most often tout are graduation rates and attendance. Both had fallen since Dr. Santelises took over in July of 2016. Her first full school year as CEO ended in the spring of 2017.

Some may blame COVID for these decreases. But the numbers were going down before the pandemic hit in 2020.

Baltimore City Schools	2017	2019	2022
Graduation Rate	70.6%	70.3%	68.6%
Attendance	87.6%	87.1%	81.8%

But these numbers didn't seem to matter. Neither did the grade-changing scandal that engulfed the school system for five years. Neither did Augusta Fells. Neither did the many calls for criminal investigations following the IG's multiple reports. Neither did the public records lawsuit City Schools lost, which cost taxpayers nearly $200,000.

Prior to this celebration, we reported on entire city schools where zero students scored proficient in any state testing. We interviewed teachers who said students were graduating without the ability to read their own diplomas. We spoke with desperate parents, like Gregory Gray, Ciara Ford and Tiffany France, pleading for their children to be properly educated. But none of that seemed to matter.

Remember this chart from the National Assessment of Educational Progress (NAEP), which shows Baltimore's drastic decline in test scores compared to America's large city average? Much of this decline happened during Dr. Santelises' tenure. In 2009, Baltimore City's total average score for math and reading was 10 points below the national large city average. In 2022 (when the event was held), Baltimore was 21 points below the national large city average. But this also didn't appear to matter.

NAEP Scores	2009	2019	2022
Baltimore City	231	226	218
Large City Average	241	244	239

And keep in mind that in 2022, of all the students in Baltimore City Schools who took the state math exam, just seven percent scored proficient. You read that correctly, 93 percent of Baltimore students who took the state assessments in 2022 were NOT proficient in math. And that year, the district's budget exceeded $1.5 billion in taxpayer money.

Yet, none of that mattered. On July 5, 2022, Baltimore City's elected officials sent a strong message to the public that they were happy with their school system.

"On behalf of the people of Baltimore," stated a jovial Mayor Scott, "I commend you for your continuing commitment to the education and development of our young people, signed by myself, Mayor Brandon Scott."

After the mayor presented Dr. Santelises with an award for excellence, she was persuaded by the public officials on stage to address the media, which was baited to attend with an announcement regarding summer learning.

"The only way I knew this was not about summer learning," explained an emotional Dr. Santelises, "is when my husband and two of my daughters walked through the door. That was the giveaway."

"Lou, baby, I love you," she said, acknowledging her husband in the audience.

"He is very reserved," she continued, fighting back tears. "He's learned patience. He does not punch members of the press in the nose."

The city leaders behind her burst out in laughter.

This time, Santelises did not mention me by name when referencing her husband punching journalists.

A few days after Santelises was praised by Baltimore's elected leaders, I received a call. The inspector general's report on grade changing had indeed been referred to various law enforcement agencies, as the Governor requested. According to the IG, many Baltimore City students received Maryland high school diplomas they did not earn. For a student to graduate, school administrators signed state government forms certifying that all legal graduation requirements were met. If the student didn't meet those requirements and still graduated, is that not fraud?

Though similar to the Augusta Fells scandal, no charges were filed. It sort of makes you wonder, what would a school actually have to do for someone to be arrested for educational or fiscal malpractice?

I don't know the answer. But what I do know is that Dr. Santelises, since that 2022 surprise celebration, has received multiple contract extensions, earning nearly $500,000 a year in total annual compensation.

Viewer Voicemail: FOX45/Project Baltimore Tipline:

"I am a teacher. When you teach, you are damned if you do, damned if you don't. I currently have a student in my class who has not completed a single writing task this year. He spends five minutes on a math test at most. I send emails to his mother every week. Guess what? Because this kid is ESL, we can't have him repeat the grade. How does this help him to be successful later? He is reading at a first-grade level, cannot even add or subtract, and could not answer a single question about the science or social studies units from this year.
I believe we are going too far in the other direction. In reacting to students being held back because of race or language, we are advancing students who do not have the tools to be successful in higher grades. It is hard to teach these days because everyone is only too happy to blame the teacher. And if I am not allowed to hold a kid back when he has learned nothing this year, then what will his teacher next year do with him?"

CHAPTER 15

IT'S SO BALTIMORE

The longer I report on public education, the more I believe that *McDonalds* was correct, "*Everything* is about data. And data is money." So, if that is indeed true, let's look at the numbers.

I assembled the chart that follows to illustrate the performance of Baltimore City Public Schools over the first eight years I've been with Project Baltimore. All of the data comes from city, state, and federal databases and represents the most updated information available at the time of this book's publication. It's an eight-year snapshot of the district.

	2017	2018	2019
Budget	$1,319,676,513	$1,313,742,798	$1,327,506,374
Enrollment	82,354	80,592	79,297
Cost Per Student	$16,204	$16,301	$16,740
Graduate Rate	70.65	72.00%	70.33%
SAT Average Scores (compostite)	910	916	887
Mean AP Grade per Exam	2.14	2.15	2.11
Attendance	87.60%	87.30%	87.10%
Dropout Rate	15.93	14.98	15.88
Chronic Absenteeism	30%	40%	42%
College Enrollment	48%	49%	53%
NAEP	2009	2019	2022
Baltimore City	231	226	218
Large City Average	241	244	239
PARCC State Testing: Math	11.8%	12.7%	13.0%
PARCC State Testing: English	16.0%	17.7%	18.9%
MCAP State Testing: Math			
MCAP State Testing: English			
Average Teacher Salary	$68,343	$69,263	$69,908
Instructional Teachers	5149	4910	4930
Average Principal Salary	$118,843	$118,592	$121,050
Director-Level Salary (admin)	$107,576	$107,590	$110,904
% of Teachers < 5 yrs Experience	36	34.7	36.2
Administrative Staff Employed	711	696	730
Total Staff Employed	9,637	9,160	9,256

2020	2021	2022	2023	2024	Total Budget ('17–'24)
$1,351,619,225	$1,526,983,389	$1,731,689,085	$1,704,864,429	$1,786,785,493	$12,062,867,306
79,187	77,856	77,807	75,995	75,811	
$17,068	$19,612	$22,256	$22,443	$23,568	
69.97%	69.20%	68.65%	70.57%	70.98%	
892	977	875	866	867	
2.16	2.07	1.98	1.83	2.09	
87.90%	80.60%	81.80%	83.60%	85.00%	
13.09	12.51	17.79	19.27	19.07	
36%	49%	58%	54%	48%	
47%	46%	43%	48%		
2024					
220					
239					
No Testing - Covid	Limited Testing - Covid				
No Testing - Covid	Limited Testing - Covid				
No Testing - Covid	Limited Testing - Covid	7.0%	8.8%	10.2%	
No Testing - Covid	Limited Testing - Covid	22.4%	26.0%	27.7%	
$72,478	$73,657	$75,675	$77,769	$77,106	
4932	5063	5109	5008	5149	
$127,685	$136,052	$136,885	$142,730	$142,864	
$109,898	$113,455	$116,805	$124,442	$130,359	
36.6	37.1	37.6	36.4	38.2	
713	738	755	817	891	
9,398	9,669	9,779	10,123	10,874	

As an investigative journalist, this is how I assemble many reports. I pull various data points from different locations and analyze what I see. These data tell a lot of stories.

Let's start at the top of the chart and work our way down.

At first, you can't help but notice the extreme increase in spending compared to enrollment. The budget has increased by nearly half a billion dollars as enrollment has fallen by eight percent. That has caused an incredible surge in the cost per pupil ratio.

Look at that! From 2017 to 2024, spending per student went up 45 percent. In 2017, the district spent $16,204 per student. By 2024, the district was spending $23,568 per student. When updated U.S. Census numbers are released, that figure will continue to be one of the highest in the nation for large school systems.

What you see below the "Cost Per Student" row details what taxpayers have received for that increased investment. The graduation rate is nearly identical. Meanwhile, SAT scores, attendance rates and the mean AP grade per exam have decreased. What has increased are the dropout rate and chronic absenteeism. The college enrollment rate is unchanged.

Overall, the district's academic performance is noticeably worse after eight years. But the funding continues to increase at staggering rates.

As a journalist, whenever I mention this data to school system officials or elected leaders in the city, they always blame COVID. And it's certainly true, the response to the pandemic affected public education. But that doesn't explain the National Assessment of Educational Progress (NAEP) scores.

The entire country dealt with the COVID pandemic, and according to NAEP, Baltimore City performed far worse than the national average for large city school systems. To quickly recap, NAEP is known as The Nation's Report Card. Every couple of years, the federal government tests student proficiency rates in all 50 states and certain cities. This allows us to compare regional levels of achievement. From 2009 to 2024, Baltimore City's average scores in math and reading are down a whopping 11 points. The large city average is down just two points.

NAEP suggests that Baltimore's problems are not rooted in COVID. And if you look at the district's other student performance metrics prior to COVID, that seems to be the logical conclusion. The graduation rate,

SAT scores, the mean AP grade per exam, attendance, the dropout rate, and chronic absenteeism were all heading in the wrong direction in 2019, the year before the COVID pandemic hit. However, if you're a school official or politician who supports the district's current power and funding structure, COVID is the easy way out, and likely will be for years to come.

Since we just analyzed federal test scores, let's now look at state assessments. What you'll notice in the chart is that Maryland, in 2020, changed standardized tests from PARCC (Partnership for Assessment of Readiness for College and Careers) to MCAP (Maryland Comprehensive Assessment Program).

The number you see for each assessment references the percentage of students districtwide who tested proficient that particular year. For example, in 2024, 10.2 percent of students in Baltimore City tested proficient in math, and 27.7 percent of students tested proficient in English Language Arts.

In other words, nearly 90 percent of students were NOT proficient in math, while nearly three-quarters of students were NOT proficient in English. If those numbers aren't alarming enough, keep in mind that taxpayers gave City Schools more than $1.7 billion for those results.

If you look at the PARCC and MCAP results, you'll notice English scores have increased since 2017, while math scores have decreased. The problem with comparing these results is that the tests are different. And the timing of the test change is a bit peculiar.

Remember the Blueprint for Maryland's Future? We discussed it in an earlier chapter. The state law increased public school funding by $32 billion in its first 10 years and then $4 billion every year after that. And it just so happens the Blueprint coincided with the change in the state test.

Maryland switched from PARCC to MCAP in 2020. The Blueprint was initially passed by the state legislature in—you guessed it—2020. Then-Governor Larry Hogan vetoed the legislation in 2020, saying it simply cost too much and there weren't enough accountability measures. But his veto didn't matter. In the following legislative session in 2021, the state legislature overrode the veto, and the bill became law.

From an accountability standpoint, it's hard for journalists or the public to hold lawmakers culpable for student success when the state test changes. How can we possibly know if the additional funding given to schools increased student achievement when the students take differ-ent tests? Comparing pre-Blueprint proficiency rates to post-Blueprint proficiency rates can be like comparing apples to oranges.

It's almost as if politicians hedged their bets. They give schools more tax dollars and then shelter those schools from criticism by adjust-ing accountability metrics. This potential political strategy became most apparent when Maryland adjusted its high school graduation requirements.

Warning: As a taxpayer or parent, you may find the following infor-mation upsetting.

There is no doubt, the most important educational metric for any school system is its four-year high school graduation rate. All other forms of student achievement, such as state test scores, attendance rates, and dropout rates, feed into the graduation rate.

In 2019, the year prior to Maryland's legislature initially passing the Blueprint, to receive a high school diploma, Maryland students had three graduation requirements: earn 21 course credits, complete 75 service hours and pass state assessments in the four main subjects (Algebra I, English 10, Government, Life Sciences.)

From 2020 to 2023, due to the COVID pandemic, students no lon-ger had to pass state assessments to graduate. They just needed to take them. And starting in 2024, new standards took effect again.

For a majority of the class of 2024, Maryland students will only have to pass two requirements to graduate—21 credits and 75 service hours. State assessments will now count for 20% of a student's final grade for that subject. But students in Maryland are no longer required to pass the state assessment tests to graduate. In other words, students can now receive a Maryland high school diploma without proving they are profi-cient in math or English.

The Maryland State Department of Education told us the change was made because "high-stakes exit exams disproportionately and negatively impact minority and economically disadvantaged students, reducing their likelihood of graduating from high school." The statement continued, saying that a "student's course grade is a stronger predictor of college and career success than performance on standardized assessments."

But if easing graduation requirements is such a great idea, why was it not done sooner?

"I think that's counterproductive," believes Desmond Stinnie.

Stinnie is a Baltimore City Schools father who ran into significant problems with the quality of his daughter, Xaviera's, education.

In 2020, Xaviera graduated from high school, but not from just any high school. She was an honor student and soccer star at Baltimore Polytechnic Institute. Poly, as it's known, is considered the premier public high school in Baltimore City.

"She's accomplishing so much more than her old man for such a young age," Stinnie told me with pride. "She is amazing."

When Xaviera graduated in 2020, Poly had a graduation rate greater than 95 percent, one of the best in Maryland. Seventy-seven percent of its students tested and scored proficient in English that year. Fifty-four percent tested proficient in math. Both are the highest scores in the Baltimore city area.

But soon after graduation, Desmond watched his daughter's bright future nearly fall apart. Xaviera enrolled as a cadet at one of the United States military academies.

"When she graduated, did you think she was prepared to go to a military academy?" I asked him.

"Absolutely," he responded. "There was no indication that she wasn't."

Stinnie says that when his daughter arrived as a cadet, she quickly fell behind and was placed on academic probation. She was in danger of failing out of college.

"That was the moment we realized that the foundation wasn't built at all," he told me. "And we had a very false sense of superiority, having the grades that we had and the academic praise that she got from city schools."

Stinnie says the academy had to create a special math remediation course to help his daughter stay in school.

"Were you shocked to learn that your daughter was so far behind in her education?" I asked him.

His eyes widened, "It was beyond shock. We never thought basic math would be the stress in her life for those sixteen months that she was on academic probation."

Xaviera worked her way off academic probation. But Stinnie worries about the other students, especially after Maryland changed its graduation requirements. A change he fears could result in more graduates not being prepared.

Added Stinnie, "And I think if we lower our standards, that's at the detriment of the children."

I followed up on his last point, "Do you think this is lowering the standards?"

"Well," he replied, "any time you got to do less to get to the same result, I think you're taking a hit on your standards. I think we're setting them up (students) to fail."

I opined, "But graduation rates will probably go up because there are fewer requirements."

Stinnie nodded. "And we talked about that false sense of superiority. We thought we were ready. And then, when it became game time against high-level competition, we weren't ready. And that could have been disastrous."

Now, let's go back to the City Schools' achievement chart. Look at the graduation rates compared to math and English proficiencies. In 2022, for example, seven percent of Baltimore City students scored proficient in math. Yet, the graduation rate that year was 68 percent. Does that make sense to you?

And now, moving forward in Maryland, students don't need to test proficient in *any* subject to receive a high school diploma. But let's further examine the newsworthy timing of that change.

As I mentioned, starting in 2020, students no longer had to pass course assessments to graduate from high school. What else happened in 2020? Yes, the pandemic happened. But also, the state legislature initially passed the Blueprint for Maryland's Future.

Here's the point: Maryland politicians passed a law that pumps billions of additional tax dollars into public education. Parents and taxpayers were promised that the increased funding would lead to improved academic outcomes. Simultaneously, the state lowered the requirements to receive a high school diploma, all but ensuring that graduation rates will increase and statewide educational data will improve.

The bet has been hedged.

When the graduation rate increases, how will the public know the reason? Will the increase be the result of additional funding? Will it be because the state made it easier for students to graduate? Could there be another reason? We'll never know—likely by design.

But I guarantee you this, in my experience as an education reporter, the schools and their political allies who lobbied heavily for the additional funding will always credit the "investment" that taxpayers made in their schools. That will inevitably be followed by requests for further "investment." And those politicians who want to keep their jobs will be happy to deliver. Educational employee organizations, such as the teachers' union, administrators' unions and AFSCME (American Federation of State, County and Municipal Employees) are the most powerful political forces in Maryland. So, in other words, the schools will continue to get more money.

And speaking of money, let's examine in the final section of the chart how most of that money is spent. These numbers speak for themselves.

As the performance of the school system has noticeably declined, the pay of its employees has significantly increased. From 2017 to 2024, teachers got about a 13 percent pay increase. Principals got a 20 percent pay increase. Director-level positions got a nice 21 percent pay increase.

District administrators are doing very well, financially. And there are more of them. As the number of students in the district has decreased by eight percent, the number of "administrative staff" has increased by more than 25 percent. Meanwhile, the number of teachers stayed the same at 5,149.

High administrative costs have been a main criticism of Baltimore schools for decades. According to the 2024 U.S. Census, Baltimore has the 5th highest administrative costs per student among the nation's 100 largest districts. Massive amounts of money are going into the pockets of administrators instead of going into the classrooms.

But it's not just administrative staff prospering from public education tax dollars. Look at the chart line, "Total Staff Employed." Over eight years, Baltimore City Schools added 1,237 employees to educate 6,543 fewer students. More adults are educating fewer students, with mostly declining academic results.

Yet, year after year, the district's budget expands to reward a greater number of employees with greater amounts of taxpayer dollars, regardless of educational outcomes. And it's just allowed to happen with little, if any, pushback from the elected officials who fund the school system with your money.

The makings of a failure factory.

The final number we'll discuss is found in the column, "Total Budget ('17–'24)." Everything you have read in this book, and all the data you see in the chart, happened between the years of 2017 and 2024. During that time span, the district has maintained the same leadership under the same CEO. And within those eight school years, taxpayers have given Baltimore City Public Schools more than $12 billion in total funding—$12 BILLION!

With that number in mind, ask yourself two questions. First, who was that money intended to benefit most—the students who attend the schools, or the adults employed by them?

While you think about your answer, schedule a trip to West Baltimore. Observe for yourself what has happened to this city in recent decades. The blight. The crime. The decay. In 1920, Baltimore was thriving as America's 7th largest city. By 2024, it had tumbled to 30th in population, with thousands of residents still fleeing most every year.

Now, ask yourself . . . Who did that $12 billion *actually* benefit most?

ABOUT THE AUTHOR

Chris Papst is the lead investigative reporter for Project Baltimore, Fox45 News' ongoing investigation into Maryland's public education system. He is a national award-winning reporter and best-selling author.

As an investigative reporter, Chris's work has led to the passing of state laws, criminal convictions and court rulings that have set legal precedent throughout Maryland. As an author, his book, *Capital Murder*, hit #1 on Amazon in three categories. His second book, *Devolution*—a novel—was released in the summer of 2016.

During his career, Chris's work has received awards of recognition from institutions such as the Maryland General Assembly, the Maryland Office of the Comptroller and the Maryland Office of the Inspector General for Education. In 2023, Chris received the Vanguard Award from the Maryland State Conference NAACP. One year later, he received the Excellence in Education Advocacy Award from the Randallstown Chapter of the NAACP.

Chris's investigative reports have been recognized with some of journalism's top national honors, including an Emmy Award for investigative reporting from the National Academy of Television Arts and Sciences.